Microsoft
Surface

JONI BLECHER

 Peachpit Press

Visual QuickStart Guide
Microsoft Surface
Joni Blecher

Peachpit Press
www.peachpit.com

To report errors, please send a note to errata@peachpit.com.
Peachpit Press is a division of Pearson Education.

Editor: Clifford Colby
Development editor: Robyn G. Thomas
Production editor: Myrna Vladic
Compositor: Danielle Foster
Copyeditor: Scout Festa
Tech editor: Mark Davis
Indexer: Valerie Haynes Perry
Cover Design: RHDG / Riezebos Holzbaur Design Group, Peachpit Press
Interior Design: Peachpit Press
Logo Design: MINE™ www.minesf.com

ISBN-13: 978-0-321-88732-0
ISBN-10:   0-321-88732-8

9 8 7 6 5 4 3 2 1

Printed and bound in the United States of America

Acknowledgments

"It takes a village" doesn't just apply to rearing children; I have learned through this project that it also applies to writing books. First, I'd like to thank Matt Rotter, my rock, for his kindness, motivation, and all-around awesomeness. It is he who introduced me to Mark Davis, the tech editor of this book. Mark's 20 years of experience developing custom Microsoft software and his most recent work as a Windows 8 software developer have proved invaluable in this project. I truly appreciate his wealth of knowledge and effortless way of connecting the tech dots. Then there's the amazing Peachpit team: Cliff Colby, who spearheaded the project, created the dream team and brought the book to fruition; Robyn Thomas, who is an impressive editor, kept the book moving along; and Scout Festa, whose attention to detail is inspiring. Finally, I'm fortunate enough to be surrounded by friends and family who provided encouragement and support in a multitude of ways while I was writing this book, and to all of you I say, "Thank you, thank you, thank you!"

Bio

Joni Blecher has been writing about mobile technology since the days before cell phones had color displays and keyboards. While serving as editorial director of LetsTalk.com, she reviewed countless mobile devices and apps and also designed how-to videos to help consumers maximize their phone experience. At CNET, Joni edited mobile-centric columns and reviews while also writing the Cell Phone Diva column, where she answered technical, practical, and etiquette questions about all things mobile. Visit her at JoniBlecher.com or on Twitter at @JoniBlecher.

Contents at a Glance

Table of Contents

Introduction

Congratulations on getting a Surface tablet. The tablet will change the way you think about Microsoft Windows and may even change the way you think about tablets. It has a new interface and a completely re-designed way to interact with apps. Depending on the model you got, it might also have come with a spacious tactile QWERTY keyboard complete with shortcut keys designed to work exclusively with the tablet. Since it can run apps like Microsoft Office and offers 7 GB of cloud-based storage via SkyDrive, it could be the only device you need to take with you when traveling.

The operating system (OS) features a graphics-based user interface (UI) on the Start screen that you navigate by using touch-based gestures and movements. The Start screen is what you will use to access and use apps. You can even run two apps simultaneously side by side on the screen using a new feature called *snapping*. The Start screen is filled with graphical squares and rectangles called *tiles* . They can be resized, moved around on the screen, and kept from appearing on the Start screen.

Ⓐ The Start screen features tiles, which launch programs and display relevant information.

You can customize the Surface tablet to see the apps you use most first. Tiles are how you access apps—just tap a tile to launch the app. Tiles can be *live*, meaning an app's information can display on the tile.

The Surface tablet is Microsoft's first entry into the quickly growing tablet market. It's a good initial effort. As is the case with any first-to-market device, there are some bugs. The good news is that the Surface tablet is updateable, and system and app updates are continually pushed out to it. If something doesn't work correctly the first time, an update just might fix it. That is also why some images or steps in this book may not mirror exactly what you see on the tablet. So be sure to install updates whenever they become available. This book will show you how to do that.

Is This Book for You?

This book is designed to help you use the Surface tablet. It includes how to use many of the Microsoft apps on the Surface tablet, such as Photos, Mail, Camera, Music, and Video. Since this is a completely new device, this book is written for anyone who wants to know how to make the most of using the Surface tablet. It provides an overview of what it offers and how to use it.

Since this book is a Visual QuickStart Guide, it provides step-by-step instructions with accompanying images to teach you how to use the Surface tablet. The images are meant as guides, so don't be concerned if what is shown in the book isn't exactly what you see on your tablet.

Although there is a physical keyboard designed specifically for the tablet, this book focuses primarily on using gestures and touch-based movements. On occasion, you'll find keyboard shortcuts for accessing features in apps. Keyboard shortcuts look like this: ⊞+C. Note that the Windows key on the keyboard (⊞) is different from the Windows button on the actual Surface tablet.

The book is written so that you don't have to read it in sequential order, but we do recommend reading the first three chapters in order. These chapters will help you customize your tablet and learn how to use it. The additional chapters will teach you how to use many of the apps that come installed on the tablet. As you read the chapters, you'll begin to see a pattern in how apps function. There are plenty of similarities that cross over between apps, and reading a few app chapters will help you understand how apps generally work.

What This Book Will Teach You

The book has 15 chapters. The first three focus on teaching you how to use the tablet. The remaining chapters focus on how to use the Microsoft apps on the tablet. Here is what you can expect to find in each chapter:

- **Chapter 1,** "Getting Started," covers the Surface tablet's specs and what you can attach to the tablet via the ports. It also teaches you how to set up and customize your tablet using PC Settings. Finally, the chapter shows you how to use the cloud-based SkyDrive app to upload files to and download files from the tablet.

- **Chapter 2,** "Navigating the Surface Tablet," teaches you to use gestures and some navigational features built into the OS to set permissions, snap apps, access the app bar (similar to the Menu bar), and share content. It also covers using and moving tiles.

- **Chapter 3,** "Working with Text," shows you how to use text boxes, switch to a stylus, and work with the various onscreen keyboard layouts.

- **Chapter 4,** "Mail and Outlook.com," explains the Mail app, as well as how to use Outlook.com to check email remotely and do more with the People and Calendar apps.

- **Chapter 5,** "Calendar," teaches you how to use the Calendar app to create and view appointments.

- **Chapter 6,** "Messaging," focuses on instant messaging (IM).

- **Chapter 7,** "People," teaches you how to add contacts to the People app from email accounts and from social media accounts such as Facebook, Twitter, and LinkedIn.

- **Chapter 8,** "Bing and Internet Explorer," explains the difference between the two apps and teaches you how to use them to perform Internet searches, surf the web, and bookmark websites.

- **Chapter 9,** "Tile-Based Apps," covers the bulk of the apps included on the tablet. The News, Finance, Travel, Sports, and Weather apps are essentially Internet feeds. This chapter teaches you how to navigate those apps and set up your own feeds.

- **Chapter 10,** "Windows Store and Games," teaches you how to navigate the Windows Store and download or purchase apps. The Games section of the chapter is a high-level look at the Games app and how to add games to it.

- **Chapter 11,** "Camera," shows you how to use the Camera app to take photos or record HD video. It also teaches you how to use its rudimentary editing features to crop photos and trim videos.

- **Chapter 12,** "Photos," functions primarily as a gallery. You will learn how to import photos from Facebook, Flickr, SkyDrive, and other folders on the Surface tablet. There are also instructions for cropping photos and trimming videos.

- **Chapter 13,** "Video," shows you how to buy and rent movies and TV shows from the Xbox Video Store. It also shows you how to use the app to view your own videos.

- **Chapter 14,** "Music," includes how to use the Music app to play music, create playlists, and purchase music from the Xbox Music Store.

- **Chapter 15,** "Maps," teaches you how to get directions, place pins on a map, and use different map views.

What's Not in This Book

Although the Surface tablet runs a version of Microsoft Windows 8, this isn't a book about using Windows 8 or about the differences between it and Windows 7. And while you can use this book to learn how to use the Start screen and tile-based apps found on the Windows 8 Pro tablet, this book isn't meant as a guide to using that tablet.

The book focuses mainly on using tiles. While there is a Desktop tile on the tablet, using the Desktop is hardly mentioned in this book. It also doesn't include more advanced Windows 8 features such as networking or setting up HomeGroups. For more detailed information on using Windows 8, check out Barrie Sosinsky's *Windows 8: Visual QuickStart Guide* (Peachpit Press, 2012).

Many of the apps covered in this book can connect with an Xbox 360. When that feature is available, we mention that it can be done but do not provide instructions on how to do it. Additionally, to get the most out of Music, Video, and Games, you will need an Xbox Live membership. The book includes information on how to access and change account settings, but it doesn't go into detail about what Xbox Live offers or how to choose a membership. Visit www.xbox.com/live for more information. That said, the book teaches you how to use those apps without a membership.

How This Book Works

The book is organized so that after reading the first three chapters you can easily skip to any chapter that focuses on the app you want to use. As noted, the first three chapters teach you how to use and customize the Surface tablet, while the remaining chapters focus on individual apps. The first section in each chapter provides a general overview and explains how to navigate the app. The next sections dive deeper into the app and teach you how to perform different tasks. The last section typically includes how to use charms to change application settings, search within an application or in other applications, or share information on the screen with a person or device. You can learn more about charms in Chapter 2.

Throughout the book, you'll find screenshots to help guide you through the step-by-step directions. Each image is labeled with a letter, such as Ⓐ, Ⓑ, Ⓒ, and so on, that corresponds to the same letter found within the text. The screenshots are there to provide a visual guide to the text-based instructions. Images in the book often include callouts or a bullet list that describe elements in the image. Refer to these images when reading a section, because they illustrate features described in the text.

At the end of each section in a chapter are tips that provide additional information related to the section. They include things like keyboard shortcuts, useful information about the section, and how to perform additional tasks that are helpful but aren't included in the section.

Conventions Used in This Book

Since Windows 8 is such a departure from Windows 7, you'll be learning a lot of new words that describe features of the OS, such as *charms*, *divider bar*, and *app bar*. The first time these words are mentioned, they appear in italics and are defined.

Placeholders appear in italics and between brackets. For example, when I say "On the Add Your [*Email Provider*] Account screen," what you'll see on your tablet will be the Add Your Gmail Account screen (or Hotmail or Yahoo or—you get the idea).

Microsoft refers to the apps used on the Surface tablet as Windows Store apps. For the sake of clarity, we refer to them in this book as *tile-based apps*. Additionally, the Windows RT tablet will run only Windows Store apps, meaning you can't install Windows 7 applications on the tablet.

Within the apps, you'll find buttons and links. When you need to tap a button, the name of the button appears in the text. Names of links are in italics.

At the center base of the Surface tablet is a Windows button. This is different from the Windows *key* on the keyboard. When referring to the Windows button on the Surface tablet, the text mentions that it's on the tablet. In keyboard shortcuts, such as ⊞+C, the ⊞ refers to the dedicated Windows key on the keyboard.

1

Getting Started

Now that you have a Surface tablet, you can customize it and make it uniquely yours. The tablet experience is tied to your Microsoft account, which is the email address and password that you use to sign in to services such as Xbox Live, SkyDrive, Messenger, and Hotmail. That's why when you first turned on your tablet, you were required to add a Microsoft account.

This chapter walks you through what to do next. It focuses on how to set up the tablet the way you want, including changing the Start screen color scheme, connecting to wireless networks, adding users, and using SkyDrive for online storage.

In This Chapter

Get to Know Your Surface Tablet Hardware

Regardless of which company made your Windows RT tablet, all tablets have a single Windows button at their base and have similar specs.

Windows button on the tablet

There is one icon on the physical tablet: the Windows button at the center of the base of the tablet. Tap it to toggle between the Start screen (the main screen, where all the tiles are located) and an active app.

Kickstand

The Surface tablet comes with a kickstand so you can place it on a table and watch a movie or do other things just by touching the screen. The kickstand was designed so that when it's extended, the rear-facing camera points straight ahead. It takes up the bottom half of the back of the tablet; just extend it, and click it into place.

Cameras

There are two cameras on the Surface tablet: one on the back and one on the front. Both cameras can record 720p HD video. The front-facing camera is a lower resolution and is meant for taking self-portraits and making video calls. The rear-facing camera has a higher resolution. You can switch between cameras in the Camera app by tapping the Switch Camera button in the app bar.

Ports

The ports on the tablet are how you connect it to other devices:

- **USB 2.0.** With a USB connection, you can connect USB peripherals such as a printer, a mouse, an external keyboard, and even a game controller. The USB 2.0 port is backward compatible to USB 1.0, so you can use those types of devices as well.

- **microSDXC.** You can add more storage to the tablet via a microSD card. The card is about the size of your pinky fingernail. The main difference between a microSD card and a microSDXC card is storage capacity. A microSD card can store up to 64 GB of data, while a microSDXC card can store up to 2 TB of data.

  Many smartphones already support microSD cards, so you can insert your phone's microSD card into the microSDXC slot on the tablet and access files stored on it. When you insert a microSD card into the tablet, it will act and look like an external drive.

- **Audio out.** This is a 3.5mm jack. You can use it to connect a standard headset or to connect the tablet to other audio peripherals that use a 3.5mm connector.

- **HD Video out.** The tablet comes with a microHDMI port that you can use to connect the tablet to other HDMI-capable devices—such as an external monitor or HDTV—so you can watch videos and other media stored on the tablet. You will need to get an additional microHDMI-to-HDMI cable to use this feature.

Optional keyboard

There is an optional keyboard available that does double duty as a cover. The keyboard has some dedicated keys that are worth noting. There's a ⊞ key on the keyboard that can be used for shortcuts. You'll find some of those keyboard shortcuts throughout the book. This ⊞ key is different than the dedicated Windows button on the tablet, which is used to toggle between an active app and the Start screen.

This external keyboard also has dedicated keys for accessing charms (see Chapter 2 for more information about charms).

TIP Store movies on a microSDXC card to conserve storage space on the tablet.

TIP If you have an optional keyboard, it can be attached so that the keyboard faces the screen, creating a laptop-style set-up. Or it can be reversed, so that if you are holding the tablet in your hand and have the keyboard cover on backward, the keys will be touching the back of the tablet.

The Start Screen

The Start screen is the main screen on the tablet. Here you will see tiles for Mail, Internet, sports, and more. Tiles are visual representations of apps. They work like the app icons found on the Windows Desktop in that you tap them to launch the app. Tiles can also be moved around the Start screen and made smaller or larger. Tiles can be "live," meaning that they can display information from that app. For example, when the Mail tile is live, it will cycle through your new messages and include the sender, subject, and first few characters of a message on the tile. When you're in an app and see squares or rectangles on the screen, these are also called tiles, but they can't be resized and typically can't be moved.

Whenever you download an app, it appears on the Start screen. However, you may need to swipe from right to left on the screen to find the new app's tile.

On the Start screen, you can customize how the tiles look, move them into groups of tiles, and even create new tile groups (see "Working with Tiles" in Chapter 2).

Think of the Start screen as your home screen. You can personalize the Start screen with colors and designs that are found in PC Settings.

PC Settings

You'll need to visit PC Settings to customize how you use the tablet, get updates, manage devices, add users, and personalize your Surface tablet.

You can access PC Settings from the Settings panel, which you get to through the Charms bar. The Charms bar is available on every screen. It's a thin bar that you access by swiping in from the right edge of the tablet. You can then tap a charm (Search, Share, Start, Devices, or Settings) for more options.

Charms are used to change application settings, search within an application, or share information on the screen with a person or device. You'll learn how to use charms and how to adjust wireless networks, sound, brightness, notifications, power, and keyboard settings.

To access PC Settings:

1. While on the Start screen, swipe in from the right edge of the tablet to reveal the Charms bar Ⓐ.

continues on next page

Ⓐ Charms bar on the Start screen

2. Tap Settings on the Charms bar. The Settings panel displays **B**.

3. Tap the *Change PC settings* link on the Settings menu to open the PC Settings options **C**.

TIP Through the Settings panel, you can access PC Settings from any application running on the Surface tablet.

TIP Unless you're prompted to save, any changes you make in PC Settings will be saved automatically.

TIP The keyboard shortcut to access the Charms bar is ⊞+C, or you can tap the dedicated shortcut key on the keyboard for the charm you want.

B Settings menu

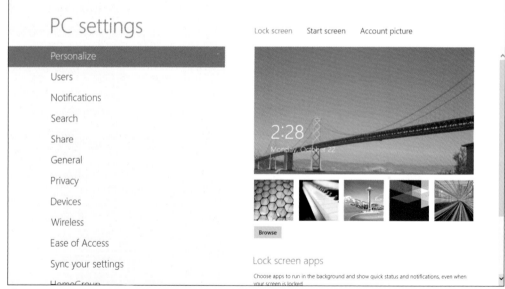

C PC Settings options

A Lock screen image options

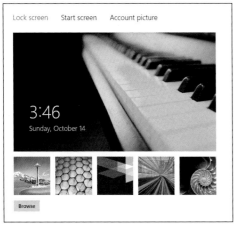

B Choosing a pre-installed picture for the lock screen

Personalize Your Tablet

When you launch PC Settings, the first option, Personalize, is highlighted. This is where you change the color scheme, pick an image for the lock screen, and choose an account picture.

To personalize the lock screen:

The lock screen is what appears on the tablet's screen when it's locked. You can choose one of the pre-installed pictures or select a picture of your own.

1. While on the Start screen, swipe in from the right edge of the tablet to reveal the Charms bar, tap Settings, and then tap the *Change PC settings* link. Tap Personalize.

2. To use a pre-installed picture, tap one of the pictures under the main image **A**. The new image appears on the main screen **B**.

3. To use a picture of your own choosing, tap the Browse button **B**. Photos stored in the Photos app appear on the screen. If you have folders already set up, tap the folder that contains the picture you want.

continues on next page

4. Tap a picture or picture folder. Tap the Choose Picture button. If you tap a picture folder, pictures in that folder will appear.

If you don't find a picture in that folder, tap the down arrow next to Files to select a picture from another folder **C**.

The chosen picture appears as the main image **D**. This is what appears when the tablet is locked.

C Folders on the tablet

D Using an existing image on the tablet for the lock screen image

ⓔ Adding notifications to the lock screen

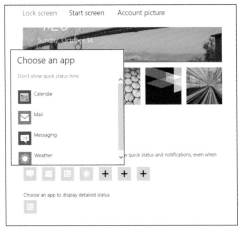

ⓕ Removing notifications from the lock screen

5. Tap the plus (+) button below the Lock Screen Apps heading. The Choose an App pop-up displays **ⓔ**.

6. Tap an application to add its notifications to the lock screen.

7. To stop an app's notifications from displaying on the lock screen, tap the icon of the app you want to remove and tap the *Don't show quick status here* link **ⓕ**.

To personalize the Start screen:

You can personalize the color scheme of the Start screen and Charms bar panels as well as the background design of the Start screen. Tap Personalize under PC Settings and tap the *Start screen* link to make changes **G**.

- **Start screen.** See how the changes will look as you make them.

- **Background designs.** Tap a box to select that design. The image appears around and behind the tiles on the Start screen.

- **Color scheme.** Change the color scheme of the tablet. Drag the arrows above and below the color bar to choose a different color scheme.

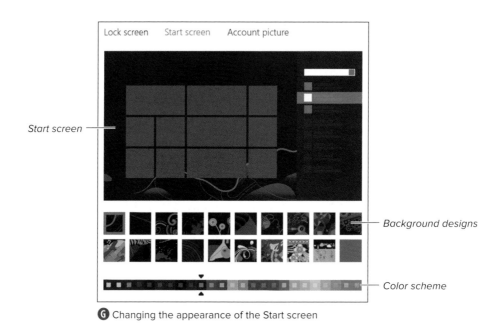

G Changing the appearance of the Start screen

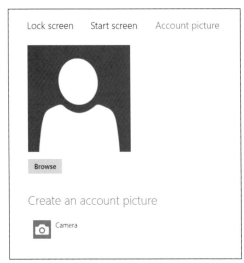

Lock screen   Start screen   Account picture

Browse

Create an account picture

Camera

H Changing the account picture

Files ∨ Pictures

Go up   Sort by name ∨

Camera Roll

Phone Photos

Windows Simulator

I Selecting a picture on your tablet

J Taking a picture with your tablet

To select an account picture:

This is the picture that displays with your account.

1. Tap Personalize under PC Settings, and tap the *Account picture* link next to the Start screen.

2. To choose a picture already on your tablet, tap the Browse button **H**. Images in the Photos app display **I**.

3. Tap a picture, or tap a picture folder and then tap a picture. Tap the Choose Image button. Tap the down arrow next to Files to choose another folder.

4. To take a picture of yourself to use as the account picture, tap the Camera button below the "Create an account picture" label, and tap the screen to take the picture. The picture displays on the screen with a resizing rectangle **J**.

5. Drag a corner circle to resize the area. You can also drag the area to reposition it.

6. Tap OK.

   or

   Tap Retake to take a new picture.

Users

The Surface tablet can support multiple users, and each user can customize PC Settings for their login. The first account associated with the tablet is the main account. Additional users can be added using Microsoft accounts or local accounts.

To add users who have a Microsoft account:

1. While on the Start screen, swipe in from the right edge of the tablet to reveal the Charms bar, tap Settings, and then tap the *Change PC settings* link. Tap Users.

2. Tap the Switch to a Microsoft Account button **A**. A screen appears, prompting you to enter the password associated with the Microsoft email account you used to set up the tablet.

3. Tap the password box and enter your password. Tap the Next button.

4. Enter the Microsoft email address you want to use to sign in, and tap the Next button. **B**.

5. Enter the password associated with the email address you entered in the previous step, and tap Next.

   If you haven't switched user accounts before, you'll be prompted to add security information. Note that this needs to be done only the first time you switch users.

6. Enter a phone number, alternate email address, and secret question and answer. Tap Next.

7. Tap Finish.

A User account settings

B Entering the Microsoft account email address

C Adding users

D Options for adding users

To add users who don't have a Microsoft account:

Users are not required to have a Microsoft email address—a local account can be created. This is a good option for creating accounts for kids.

1. Tap the Add a User (+) button on the Users screen **C**.

2. If the user you're adding has an email address that is associated with a Microsoft account, enter the email address, tap Next, and then tap Finish. Skip the following steps.

   or

   To create a local account, tap the *Sign in without a Microsoft account* link **D** and complete steps 3–5.

   continues on next page

3. Enter a user name and password, re-enter the password, and add a password hint. Tap Next **E**.

4. To turn on family safety features, tap the checkbox next to "Is this a child's account? Turn on Family Safety to get reports of their PC use."

5. Tap Finish.

To create sign-in options:

You can change your password, create a picture password that unlocks the screen, or create a PIN.

1. Tap Users in PC Settings. Tap the Change Your Password button in the Sign-in Options section **A**.

2. In the Current Password box, type your existing password, and tap Next.

3. In the New Password box, type your new password, and then re-enter it in the Re-enter Password box. Type a password hint in the Password Hint box. Tap Next.

4. Tap Finish. The Your Account screen displays.

5. Tap the Create a Picture Password button **A**.

6. Enter your password in the password box, and tap OK **F**. The Welcome to Picture Password screen displays **G**.

E Adding a user without a Microsoft account

F Confirming the existing password

G Picture password

H Selecting a picture to use as a password

I Using gestures to create a password

J Creating a PIN password

7. Tap the Choose Picture button **G**. The Files screen displays.

8. Tap a picture in the My Pictures folder. Tap Open **H**.

9. Tap the Use This Picture button **I**. Draw three gestures on the picture. Remember the gestures and their order, since they will need to be replicated to unlock the tablet. Repeat the gestures and tap Finish.

   To remove the picture password, return to PC Settings and tap Users. Tap the Remove button next to the Picture Password button.

10. Tap the Create a PIN button in PC Settings **A**. Enter a four-digit code, re-enter it in the confirmation box, and tap the Finish button **J**.

Notifications

Many apps offer notifications that alert you of things happening with the app. If you choose to turn these on, the notifications will appear for a few seconds in the upper-right corner of the screen.

For example, if Messaging is running and someone wants to chat with you, a notification appears on the Start screen asking if you want to chat with that person.

To change Notifications settings:

1. Tap Notifications in PC Settings. The Notifications panel displays.

2. Drag the slider for each app right or left to turn the notification features on or off, respectively, in that app 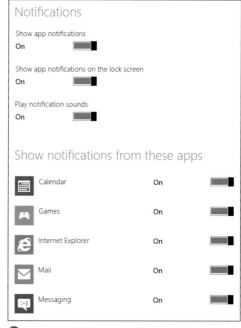.

   ▸ **Show app notifications.** Turn all notifications on or off.

   ▸ **Show app notification on the lock screen.** When in the lock screen, you can receive notifications, such as upcoming appointments and new email.

   ▸ **Play notification sounds.** Be alerted by a sound when a notification arrives.

   ▸ **Show notifications from these apps.** Select which apps can send notifications.

TIP You can also change the Notifications settings for an individual app by accessing the Settings charm while in that app.

A Notifications

A Search options

Search

To search for anything on the tablet, you'll need to access the Search charm (see Chapter 2 for more information). You can change what is searchable in the Search settings.

To change Search settings:

1. In PC Settings, tap Search to display the Search settings.

2. Drag the sliders right or left to turn search settings on or off, respectively **A**.

    ▸ **Show the apps I search most often at the top.** If this is turned on, then the three apps that appear here are the apps you search most.

    ▸ **Let Windows save my searches as future search suggestions.** Turn this on if you want recent searches to appear as search suggestions for future searches (when relevant).

    ▸ **Delete History.** Tap this button to delete your search history.

    ▸ **Use these apps to search.** Select which apps you want to be searchable.

Share

You can share items such as Internet links, movie information, and more with others via the Share charm (see Chapter 2 for more information). The Share settings manage what you can do when you open the Share panel in an app.

To change Share settings:

1. Tap Share in PC Settings to display the Share settings.

2. Drag the sliders right or left to turn the Share settings on or off, respectively **Ⓐ**.

   ▸ **Show apps I use most often at the top of the app list.** If this is turned on, the apps that appear here are the apps you use most to share items from the tablet.

   ▸ **Show a list of how I share most often.** Turn this on if you want the ways you share most to populate the Share charm. For example, if you tend to share items via email, Mail will appear in the list of Share options.

   ▸ **Items in list.** Tap the down arrow to choose how many share options you want shown. Tap the Clear List button if you want to delete your share history.

   ▸ **Use these apps to share.** Select which apps you want to use to share.

Ⓐ Share settings

General

The General settings include items that don't fall into other categories. It has settings for Time, App Switching, Touch Keyboard, Spelling, Language, Available Storage, Refresh PC, and Reinstall Windows. The list is long, so you'll need to flick up and down the screen to see all the options **Ⓐ**.

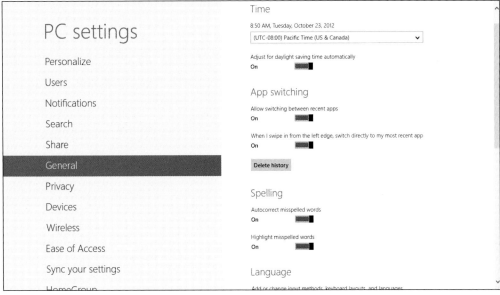

Ⓐ General settings

To set the time:

1. Tap General in PC Settings, tap the down arrow in the Time field, and flick up and down to find your time zone. Tap the time zone to select it **B**.

2. Drag the daylight saving time bar right or left to turn it on or off, respectively **C**.

To set app switching options:

With app switching, you can access running apps and bring them to the main screen from the left edge of the tablet.

- Under App Switching, drag the "Allow switching between recent apps" slider right or left to turn it on or off, respectively **D**.

- Drag the "When I swipe in from the left edge, switch directly to my most recent app" slider right or left to turn it on or off, respectively **D**. Note that the instructions in this book assume that this feature is turned off, so that when you swipe in from the left edge, you see apps that are running.

- To close all open apps, tap the Delete History button.

B Setting the time zone

C Adjusting for daylight saving time

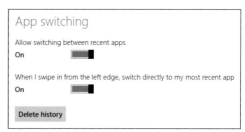

D App switching controls

Touch keyboard

Show text suggestions as I type

On

Add a space after I choose a text suggestion

On

Add a period after I double-tap the Spacebar

On

Capitalize the first letter of each sentence

On

Use all uppercase letters when I double-tap Shift key

On

Play key sounds as I type

On

Make the standard keyboard layout available

Off

E Touch keyboard settings

To set the touch keyboard options:

There's an onscreen touch keyboard that appears in the absence of a physical keyboard. Drag the sliders right or left to turn the touch keyboard options on or off, respectively **E**.

- **Show text suggestions.** Turn on to show suggestions while typing.

- **Add a space.** Turn on to add a space after you choose a text suggestion.

- **Add a period.** Turn on to add a period by double-tapping the spacebar.

- **Capitalize.** Turn on to capitalize the first letter of a sentence.

- **Use all uppercase letters.** Turn on for a caps lock feature. Double-tapping the Shift key types only uppercase letters.

- **Play key sounds.** Turn on to hear clicking sounds while you type.

- **Make the standard keyboard layout available.** There are multiple keyboard layouts available. Turn on if you want only the standard keyboard.

To set spelling and language options:

There are basic spelling correction options available. You can change the language, change the input methods, and select keyboard layouts.

1. Drag the "Autocorrect misspelled words" slider right or left to turn this option on or off, respectively 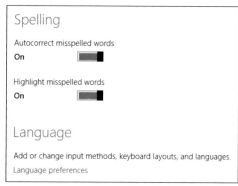.

2. Drag the "Highlight misspelled words" slider right or left to turn this option on or off, respectively **F**.

3. Tap the *Language preferences* link **F**. Tap the *Options* link **G** to see available languages.

4. Tap the *Change date, time, or number formats* link. The Region dialog box displays. Use the down arrows to change how the information is formatted on the tablet **H**.

F Spelling settings

G Choose languages

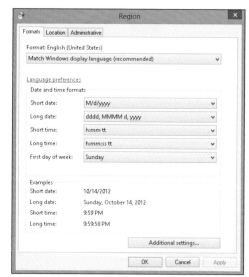

H Changing the date, time, and number formatting

Available storage

You have 412 GB available. See how much space your apps are using.

`View app sizes`

Refresh your PC without affecting your files

If your PC isn't running well, you can refresh it without losing your photos, music, videos, and other personal files.

`Get started`

Remove everything and reinstall Windows

If you want to recycle your PC or start over completely, you can reset it to its factory settings.

`Get started`

ℹ View available storage and tablet reset options.

To view the storage and reset the tablet:

To return to PC Settings from the previous instructions, swipe in from the left edge of the screen and drag the small PC Settings screen to the center of the screen. Tap General under PC Settings and swipe up.

- **Available storage.** Tap the View App Sizes button to see how much storage space each app is using ℹ.

- **Refresh your PC without affecting your files.** Tap the Get Started button to refresh the tablet without losing any of your data ℹ.

- **Remove everything and reinstall Windows.** Tap the Get Started button to completely reinstall the Windows OS ℹ.

TIP Before choosing to reinstall Windows, back up your data (this includes things like pictures, music, documents, and videos) because it will all be erased when you reinstall.

Privacy

The Privacy settings in this chapter focus on the tablet. Additional privacy options are available in apps and can be found by accessing the Settings charm while in that app.

To set Privacy options:

1. Tap Privacy in PC Settings.

2. Drag the sliders right or left to turn the options on or off, respectively 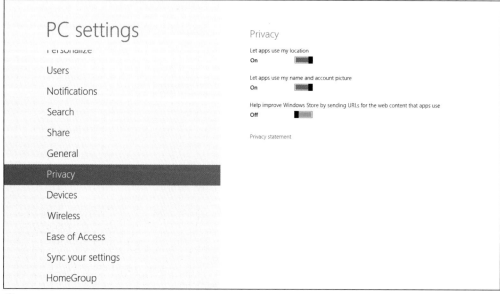.

   ▶ **Let apps use my location.** Turn on to let apps access your location.

   ▶ **Let apps use my name and account picture.** Turn on if you want your name and account picture to appear in apps.

   ▶ **Help improve Windows Store.** Turn on if you want to send URLs used by apps to the Windows Store.

PC settings

Personalize

Users

Notifications

Search

Share

General

Privacy

Devices

Wireless

Ease of Access

Sync your settings

HomeGroup

Privacy

Let apps use my location
On

Let apps use my name and account picture
On

Help improve Windows Store by sending URLs for the web content that apps use
Off

Privacy statement

Ⓐ Privacy settings

Devices

Use the Devices settings to manage devices that can connect with your tablet. You can add, remove, or rename devices in this setting.

To manage devices:

Tap Devices in PC Settings to access the devices options.

- Tap the Add a Device (+) button **A**. The tablet will look for available devices. You will then be prompted to complete the connection.

- Change the name of a device by tapping the name; a text box appears. Tap in the box, and use the keyboard to change the name. Tap the gray box around it to accept the change. Tap the X to delete the name **A**.

- To remove a device, tap the minus icon (−) **A** and then tap the Remove button in the confirmation pop-up.

A Managing devices

Wireless

Tap Wireless in PC Settings to access the wireless settings.

- Drag the Airplane Mode slider right or left to turn this feature on or off, respectively. Airplane mode is only necessary if you are using a data connection provided by a wireless carrier.

- Drag the Wi-Fi slider right or left to turn this feature on or off, respectively.

Windows Update

Tap Windows Update in PC Settings to get updates for the Windows OS. This is different from app updates; you will be notified of app updates in the Windows Store. Tap the Check for Updates Now button to see if there are any updates.

TIP **Even if there are no updates listed in Windows Update, you should still manually check for updates to the OS to make sure your tablet is up to date.**

Sync Your Settings and HomeGroup

Tap Sync Your Settings in PC Settings if you want settings such as Wi-Fi passwords and the look of the Start screen to follow you to multiple Windows 8 computers.

Tap HomeGroup in PC Settings to set up a local area network so you can share videos, music, photos, and more across devices on the network. This will also work with computers running Windows 7.

You can read more about these features in *Windows 8: Visual QuickStart Guide* (Peachpit Press, 2012), by Barrie Sosinsky.

A Desktop tile on the Start screen

B Access Bluetooth settings from the task tray.

C Bluetooth options

Bluetooth

You can connect a Bluetooth device to the tablet and share files with it. The first step is to make sure the Surface tablet is "visible," or "discoverable." Unfortunately, making your tablet visible to other Bluetooth devices isn't immediately obvious.

To turn on Bluetooth:

1. Tap the Desktop tile on the Start screen **A**.

2. Tap the up arrow in the icon task tray in the lower-right corner of the screen **B**.

3. Tap the Bluetooth icon, and tap Open Settings **C**. The Bluetooth Settings dialog box displays **D**.

4. Tap the box labeled "Allow Bluetooth devices to find this computer" **D**. The Surface tablet is now discoverable.

D Making the tablet visible (discoverable) to Bluetooth devices

To connect and pair a Bluetooth device:

Make sure the device you want to pair is visible.

1. Tap the *Change PC settings* link in the Settings panel, and tap Devices.

2. Tap the Add a Device button. The tablet will search for visible Bluetooth devices within 30 feet. Visible devices display in the Select a Device list.

3. Tap the device you want to connect to in the Select a Device list 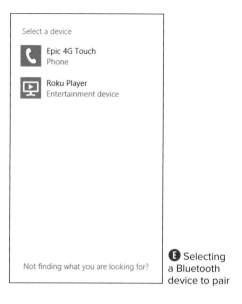.

4. A passcode appears on the tablet screen. Make sure the passcode on the screen is the same as the passcode on your Bluetooth device, and tap Yes **F**.

5. Accept the passcode on your Bluetooth device. The devices are paired, and you will see the Bluetooth device in the list of devices.

TIP You can change the name of the device by tapping it in the Devices list and typing a new name in the text box.

E Selecting a Bluetooth device to pair

F Completing the Bluetooth pairing

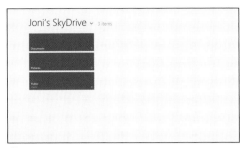

Ⓐ SkyDrive start screen

Ⓑ SkyDrive app bar

SkyDrive

Your Microsoft account comes with Sky-Drive and 7 GB of free storage space so you can store and share images, files, videos, and more in the cloud. If you plan on doing a lot of sharing from your tablet, this is one of the first things you should set up. Items placed on your SkyDrive are available from anywhere you have an Internet connection. Visit skydrive.com in an Internet browser and enter your Microsoft email account and password to access items on your SkyDrive or to store files from other devices. There are also a lot more Sky-Drive file management features available at skydrive.com.

To set up SkyDrive:

1. Tap the SkyDrive tile on the Start screen. You will see three built-in folders: Documents, Pictures, and Public **Ⓐ**.

2. Swipe up from the bottom of the screen to reveal the app bar **Ⓑ**.

   ▸ **Refresh.** Tap this button to refresh the screen. This is helpful when you've uploaded items to SkyDrive and they don't immediately appear on the screen.

   ▸ **New Folder.** Tap to create a new folder. Type a name for the folder, and tap the Create Folder button.

   ▸ **Upload.** Tap this button to upload a file to SkyDrive.

   ▸ **Details.** Tap this button to see how many items are in a folder and how much storage space they occupy. When in Details mode, the icon changes to Thumbnails. Tap the Thumbnails button to return to the main overview.

continues on next page

- **Select all.** Tap this button to select everything on the current screen.

    When you tap an item in your Sky-Drive, additional options appear on the app bar **C**.

- **Clear selection.** Tap this button to remove the check mark from the selected item.

- **Download.** Tap this button to download the item from SkyDrive.

- **Delete.** Tap this button to delete the item from SkyDrive.

- **Open with.** Tap this button to select an application to open the item with.

To upload a file:

1. Tap the Upload button in the app bar.

2. Tap the down arrow next to Files to pick a folder that contains an item you want to upload **D**.

3. Tap and hold the file you want to upload until a check mark appears in the upper-right corner of the image box **E**.

4. Tap the Add to SkyDrive button. The items upload.

C Additional SkyDrive app bar options

D Choosing the folder that contains the item you'd like to upload

E Selecting items to upload

To download a file:

1. Tap and hold a file you want to download until a check mark appears on the file, and tap the Download button in the app bar .

continues on next page

🄵 Selecting items to download

2. Tap the down arrow next to Files to display folders on the tablet. Tap the folder that you want to download the item to, and tap the Choose This Folder button . The item downloads into that folder.

TIP Select multiple items to upload to the tablet or download from the tablet by tapping and holding them until a check mark displays on each.

TIP If you want to upload items to a particular folder on SkyDrive, tap that folder and then tap Upload in the app bar.

TIP When you view SkyDrive in a web browser, there are many more things you can do, such as search the drive and even drop files into individual folders.

G Selecting the folder you want to download items to

Navigating the Surface Tablet

The Microsoft Surface Windows RT tablet provides a new and inventive user experience. Nothing that you know about using Windows on the desktop applies on the tablet. For example, the menu bar at the top of an application, which gives you more options for doing things in the app, is gone. The "idea" of the menu bar still exists, but it looks different and you access it in a completely new way.

The good news is that once you've mastered a few basic navigation techniques, using the tablet will be a breeze. You may even find yourself saying, "What took them so long to change it?"

In This Chapter

Touch Gestures

Since the tablet is primarily a touch-based device, you can use gestures to interact with it. Many of the things you would normally use a mouse to do can be done with the touch of a finger:

- **Swipe up from bottom of screen.** Swipe a finger up from the bottom edge of the screen to reveal the app bar.

- **Swipe right from left edge of screen.** Swipe a finger in from the left edge of the screen to reveal a list of running apps. A basic swipe cycles through the apps running on the tablet. To snap apps, drag a running app right while in another application, and the divider bar will appear. Release to snap the app.

- **Swipe left from right edge of screen.** Swipe a finger in from the right edge of the screen to reveal the Charms bar.

- **Swipe down from top of screen.** Some apps have an additional app bar at the top of the screen. Swipe a finger down from the top edge of the screen to reveal the top app bar. This feature is not available in all apps.

- **Pinch.** Touch the screen with two fingers and then pinch them together to zoom in. This is also how you access semantic zoom, which makes a window of large tiles that extend past the screen area (you would have to flick to see all of them) much smaller so you can see everything in one screen.

- **Expand.** Touch the screen with two fingers and then spread them apart to zoom out. Use this to remove a semantic zoom or to change the small tiles or images on the screen to large tiles or images.

- **Tap.** Select something by tapping it once. This is the equivalent of a single mouse-click.

- **Double-tap.** Tap an item twice to perform the same action as double-clicking a mouse.

- **Tap and hold.** To achieve the same action as a right-click, tap and hold an item and tap next to it with a second finger. This can also be done by tapping and holding an item until you see a blue ring around the item, and then releasing.

- **Drag.** Move an item by touching it and then dragging your finger across the screen in the direction you want the item to move.

- **Flick.** Quickly flick your finger up, down, left, or right to move all the items on the screen in that direction.

The following gesture is not common on the tablet, but it may be available in some apps.

- **Rotate.** Tap and hold an item on the screen, and pivot around it with a second finger; or tap and hold with two fingers, and rotate both fingers clockwise or counterclockwise.

Switch Between Apps

The entire surface of the tablet is dynamic. That means that even the edges of the screen have something to reveal.

The left side of the tablet is for switching and cycling through apps. If you do a long swipe from the left of the screen to the right, you'll cycle through all the running apps. If you do a shorter swipe and hold, you'll see the *switcher*, which is a list of apps you currently have open. You can access this panel in an app or from the Start screen.

To use the left-side panel:

1. To reveal the switcher, swipe in from the left edge and hold Ⓐ.

    or

    Press ⊞+Tab on the keyboard.

2. To access any app that is already running, tap the smaller version of it in the left panel.

3. To hide the left panel, tap anywhere on the screen.

Ⓐ Switcher displaying running apps

To open and manipulate apps:

If you have multiple apps open, you can use the left panel to view two apps simultaneously or open an already running app. This feature is called *snapping*.

- To open a running app, swipe in from the left edge of the screen and drag the app to the middle of the screen.

- To display two apps simultaneously on the screen, swipe from the left edge of the screen to the right. You will see a smaller version of the app that you are snapping. When you see a vertical bar with three dots in the middle (this is called the *divider bar*), release. The new app snaps to a third of the screen **B**.

Snapped secondary app

Divider bar   Primary app

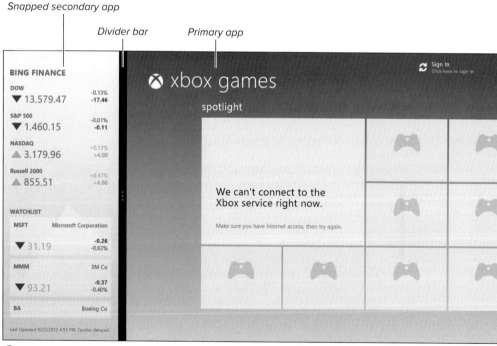

B Snapping an app

- To have the new app take over the majority of the screen and reduce the other app to a third, drag the divider bar to the right **C**. Stop when the app on the right takes up a third of the screen.

- To remove the app on the right from the screen, drag the divider bar to the right and off the screen.

- To close an app, swipe from the left edge to display the left panel, then drag the app from the left panel to the bottom of the screen.

TIP The app that appears at the bottom of the screen is the one that was used most recently.

TIP Press the Windows button at the base of the tablet to return to the home screen or to go from the Start screen to the most recently used running app.

C The secondary app becomes more prominent on the screen.

The App Bar

Think of the app bar as a menu bar like those at the top of applications such as Microsoft Word, Microsoft Excel, or just about any other application you've used on a computer. You'll need to access the app bar to perform actions that you used to find in the menu bar.

To access the app bar:

1. With an app open on the screen, swipe up from the bottom of the screen. The app bar displays **Ⓐ**.

2. To hide the app bar, swipe down from the top of the app bar.

   or

   Press Esc on the keyboard (virtual or real).

To display the top app bar:

Some applications, such as Internet Explorer, have a top app bar as well as a bottom app bar.

1. With an application open, swipe down from the top of the screen. The top app bar displays **Ⓑ**.

2. To make the app bar disappear, tap Refresh.

TIP The app bar is available in every application and is always accessed the same way.

TIP To access the app bar via keyboard shortcut, press **⊞**+Z.

Ⓐ The app bar

Ⓑ Top app bar

Charms

Charms are an essential part of the Windows 8 RT experience. They are used to change application settings, search within an application or in other applications, or share information on the screen with a person or another device. They can be accessed from every app and from the home screen. If you get a real keyboard with the tablet, it will have dedicated keys for each of the charms: Search, Share, Start, Devices, and Settings; the virtual keyboard does not have dedicated keys.

To access charms:

1. Swipe from the right edge of the screen toward the center. The Charms bar appears **A**.

2. To select a charm, tap it.

3. To hide the Charms bar, touch it and swipe right.

   or

   Tap anywhere on the screen outside the Charms bar.

A Charms bar

To use the Search charm:

The Search charm is the quickest and easiest way to find something on the Surface tablet. In addition to searching within the open app, you can use it to search for anything on the tablet or on the Internet. For example, if you're in the People app, launch the Search charm, type a name in the search box, and tap the Search icon. It will search for anyone matching that name. The Search charm can also be used to search for information in other apps.

1. To search for apps from the Start screen, select the Search charm from the Start screen **B**. If you highlight another app in Start Search, you will be performing the search in that particular app.

2. Begin typing what you want to find. As you type, the search results narrow **C**.

   The number of available items for your search will appear next to each category.

3. To change the category that's being searched, tap the category name, such as Settings, Files, and so on **D**.

B The Search charm

C Begin typing your query in the search box.

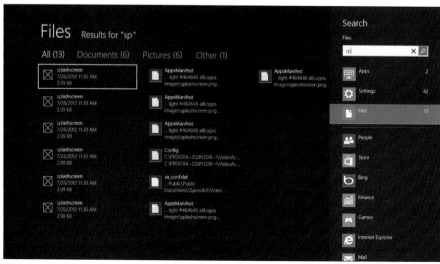

D Search results by category

E Search results from the Windows Store

F Search suggestions

To launch apps from Start Search:

Although the Search charm has parameters for what it will search based on the context from which it was launched, you can still use it to launch and search in other apps. For example, if you're in the Start screen and want to quickly find something on the Internet, tap Internet in the Search panel, type your query in the search box, and tap the Search icon. This will launch the Internet application with the search results.

1. Tap an app that you want to search **E**. Type a query in the search box and tap the Search icon. The results for the initial search query appear on the screen in the app that you are searching.

2. Enter a new term in the search box **F**. It will display the results available in that application as well as predict what you may be looking for based on the entered text.

To use the Share charm:

The Share charm does exactly what it sounds like—it quickly shares something from an app with someone. What can be shared will vary by app, but generally it's a link or a file or content from the app. Each application will have its own permissions about what can be shared and what method it can use to share something. In this example, we'll look at sharing a picture.

1. Launch the Photos app from the Start screen **G**. The Pictures library displays.

2. Click the photo that you want to share **H**.

3. Open the Charms bar and tap the Share charm.

   The methods available to share the photo appear.

4. Select how you want to share the photo. For this example, tap Mail **I**. (Even if you don't have the Mail app set up yet, as long as you have this information in the People app it will appear on the Share screen.) A message with the photo already attached appears.

5. Enter the email address to which you want to send the photo **J**. Tap Add a Subject if you want to add a subject line. Tap the Send icon (it looks like an envelope) in the upper-right corner to share the photo.

Photos app

G Photos app on the Start screen

H A selected photo

I Using the Mail app to share a photo

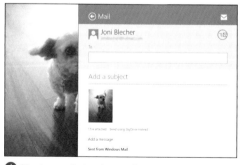

J Sharing a photo via email

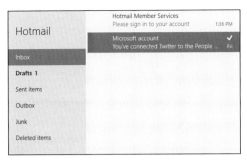

K Selecting an email

L Selecting the Devices charm on the Charms bar

M Available devices for this app

N Sending information to another device

To use the Start charm:

The Start charm works like the dedicated Windows button at the base of the tablet.

- To return to the Start screen, tap Start.
- To return to the most recently used app when the Start screen is displayed, tap the Start charm.

To use the Devices charm:

The Devices charm can send items to other devices (such as printers) that may be connected to the tablet. If an app is compatible with another device on the network, this is an easy way to connect with it. For this example, we will use Mail (see Chapter 4 to learn more about Mail).

1. Launch Mail from the Start screen.

2. Select an email you want to print K.

3. Tap Devices in the Charms bar L.

4. Tap the *More* link to see other devices that will work with this app M.

5. Choose the device to which you want to connect. For this example, tap Microsoft XPS Document Writer N. Review the settings, and then tap Print (or tap the back arrow to cancel).

To use the Settings charm:

The Settings charm allows you to access settings for the tablet and for any app from which you open it. To customize and change how things work on the tablet, you'll need to tap Change PC Settings.

With the Start screen displayed, launch the Charms bar and tap Settings  to gain access to the following options:

- To change what information appears in the tiles on the screen or to show administrative tools, tap Tiles **P**.

- For answers to commonly asked questions about using the Start menu, tap Help **Q**.

O The Start screen Settings panel

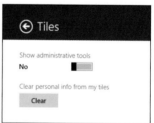

P Changing Tiles settings

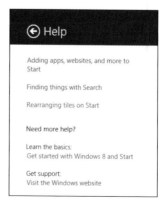

Q Using the tablet Help

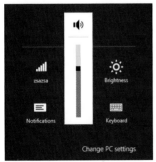

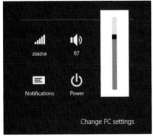

■ To locate available Wi-Fi connections, turn Airplane Mode on or off, or turn the wireless antenna on or off, tap Networks **R**.

■ To adjust the volume of the speaker, tap the speaker button and drag the scroll bar up or down **S**.

■ To adjust the screen's brightness level, tap the Brightness button and drag the scroll bar up or down **T**.

continues on next page

R Selecting a Wi-Fi network

S Adjusting the volume

T Adjusting the brightness of the screen

- You can hide notifications that appear on the screen for 1 hour, 3 hours, or 8 hours by tapping the Notifications icon and tapping one of the options in the pop-up ⓤ.

- To put the tablet to sleep, shut it down, or restart it, tap Power ⓥ.

- To change the type of virtual keyboard being used, tap Keyboard. Tap Touch Keyboard and Handwriting Panel to display the touchscreen keyboard ⓦ.

TIP Press Esc on the keyboard to hide the Charms bar.

TIP Search automatically searches everything related to where you launched the Search panel from. So if you selected to search in the Windows Store, you will see results only from the Windows Store.

TIP You can access the Search charm by pressing ⊞+Q or, on Windows 8-compatible keyboards, the dedicated Search charm key.

TIP You can access the Share charm by pressing ⊞+H or, on Windows 8-compatible keyboards, the dedicated Share charm key.

TIP You can use Microsoft XPS Document Writer to format a document before printing. Think of it as Print Preview.

TIP Turn on Airplane Mode when traveling on a plane to conserve battery life.

ⓤ Changing Notifications

ⓥ Adjusting power settings

ⓦ Onscreen keyboard

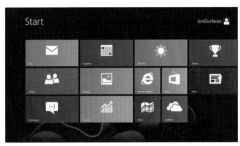

A Installed apps

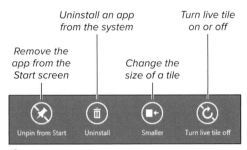

Remove the
app from the
Start screen

Uninstall an app
from the system

Change the
size of a tile

Turn live tile
on or off

B Changing the display options of a tile

Working with Tiles

Tiles are squares on the Start screen that provide access to the apps on the tablet. Tiles for Microsoft's tile-based apps can be "live." This means that if you have information loaded in the app, it will cycle through that information on the screen. For example, the pictures you have in the Photos app will cycle through the display on the Photo tile. If you don't want to see pictures of your contacts cycling through on the People app tile, you can change that behavior in the Settings charm. Apps whose tiles don't have the ability to become live aren't considered tile-based apps (instead they are standard Windows apps), and their tiles will remain static on the Start Screen; but you can change how they look and where they appear on the Start Screen.

To view tiles on the Start screen:

As you install more applications, they will appear automatically in the Start screen.

1. To display the installed apps, swipe across the screen from right to left **A**.

2. To change the size of a tile and how it is displayed on the screen, swipe up from the bottom of the screen to display the app bar **B**.

continues on next page

3. On the app bar, tap the change that you would like to make to the tile:

- **Smaller.** Tap this to change the tile from a rectangle to a square. If it's already smaller, the option will read Larger and will change a tile from a square to a rectangle.

- **Turn Live Tile On.** Tap this to have images or other information cycle through the tile on the Start screen. If the tile already has information cycling through it, the option will read Turn Live Tile Off.

- **Uninstall App.** Tap this to remove the app from the Surface tablet.

- **Unpin from Start.** Tap this to remove the tile from the Start screen.

To pin an app to the Start screen:

1. Select All Apps from the app bar on the Start screen.

2. Tap and hold the app you want to add to the Start screen **C**. Tap Pin To Start on the context menu that appears.

C Adding an app to the Start screen

D Moving tiles on the Start screen

E A new tile group

F Bird's-eye view of tiles

To move or group tiles on the Start screen:

As you install more applications, they will appear automatically in the Start screen, but that doesn't mean you need to leave them where they appear. You can move tiles individually or create a tile group.

- To move a tile, drag it to the desired location on the Start screen **D**.

- To start a new group with an existing app, drag it horizontally until you see a gray bar appear **E**. Drop the tile on the gray bar to create a new group of apps **E**. Repeat to add more tiles to the group.

To zoom out on the Start screen:

To see all the tiles available on the Start screen, tap the minus (–) button in the lower-right corner of the screen or use the zoom out gesture. This shrinks the tiles to provide a bird's-eye view **F**.

To name a tile group:

1. Tap and hold a tile group to select it. This launches the app bar **G**. Tap the Name Group option.

2. Enter a name for the group and tap Name **H**. The group's name will appear above it on the Start screen **I**.

TIP If you remove an app from the Start screen, you can still find the app by tapping All Apps on the Start screen's app bar.

TIP Once you select an app on the Start screen, you can click additional apps and tap Unpin from Start or Pin to Start to remove or add multiple apps simultaneously. If the app is already pinned, the only option will be Unpin; if the app is unpinned, the only option will be Pin.

TIP If there is only one tile in a group or column, you can remove it by unpinning it.

TIP To remove a group's name, follow the same steps to name a group and just delete the name from the Name box by clicking the X in the corner of the text field; tap Name to save the change.

G Selecting a group

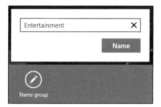

H Naming a group

I Named group on Start screen

3

Working with Text

There are four options for creating text on the Surface tablet: the onscreen keyboard, a stylus, a physical keyboard, and writing or drawing with your finger. You can also highlight text on the screen using your finger or a stylus to do things like cut, copy, and paste. Whichever you choose, it's simple to switch to another input format. This chapter walks you through the variety of keyboards available, how to insert emoticons in text fields, and how to improve handwriting recognition results.

Onscreen Keyboards

If you have a physical keyboard attached to the tablet, it will be the default method for entering text and numbers. There are two onscreen keyboard layouts: a standard QWERTY keyboard and an ergonomic layout with a numeric keypad in the middle. When there is an option on a screen to input text, tap the text area and the keyboard will appear on the screen. The onscreen keyboard displays in the bottom third of the screen, but you can scroll any app up and down to see the information obscured by the keyboard.

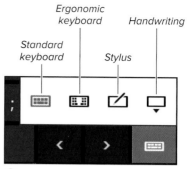

Ⓐ Changing the input method

To change keyboards:

1. When the keyboard appears, tap the keyboard icon in the lower-right corner of the screen.

2. Tap the keyboard you want to use Ⓐ, and the keyboard layout changes.

To work with the standard QWERTY keyboard:

Some standard keyboard functions, such as tabbing to indent or using punctuation, are not immediately obvious. Those features are still available **B** and accessed by pressing certain keyboard buttons.

- **Up arrow.** Tap the up arrow once to capitalize the next letter typed. Tap twice to activate cap lock mode; tap again to deactivate cap lock mode. Dedicated keys for quotes, semicolon, colon, and exclamation point appear when you double-tap the up arrow key **C**.

continues on next page

Numbers   Ctrl   Emoticons/
icons

Right/left arrows   Up arrow

B Onscreen keyboard features

C Creating capital letters and punctuation

- **Right/left arrows.** Tap to move right or left through a string of text. You can also tap the screen to place the cursor.

- **Numbers.** Tap the numbers key for numbers, more punctuation, and the Tab key **D**.

- **Emoticons/icons.** Tap the smiley face key to see emoticons **E**. Tap a key on the bottom row to see more icons relating to that category: Tap the balloon for holiday icons, the pizza for food icons, the plane for travel icons, weather for weather-related icons (phases of the moon, for example), punctuation for additional symbols, and the text-based smiley face for text-based emoticons.

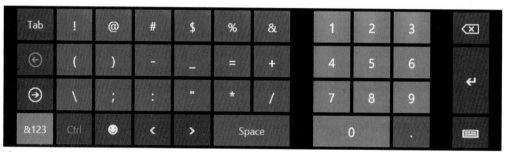

D Numbers keyboard layout

E Emoticons keyboard layout

- **Ctrl.** Tap the Ctrl button and the corresponding letter to complete the shortcuts for Select All (A), Undo (Z), Cut (X), Copy (C), and Paste (V) **F**.

To work with the ergonomic keyboard:

The ergonomic keyboard has the same features as the standard QWERTY keyboard. The main difference, besides layout, is the three dots next to the space bar on the left. Tap those dots and then tap Small, Medium, or Large in the pop-up menu to change the size of the keys **G**.

TIP Access the Cut, Copy, and Paste commands by tapping and holding in an app's text box and tapping next to it with another finger.

F Ctrl keyboard layout

G Ergonomic keyboard layout

Text and the Touchscreen

Even if you have a physical keyboard attached, many apps allow you to enter text and draw pictures using a stylus or your finger. Just start writing or drawing on the screen. Other apps will require you to switch to the stylus or handwriting options.

To switch to using a stylus or handwriting from the onscreen keyboard:

1. When the keyboard appears on the screen, tap the keyboard icon in the lower-right corner of the screen 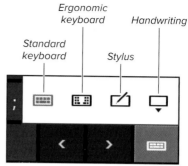.

2. To use a stylus, tap the stylus icon (it looks like a rectangle with a pen). A scribe area will appear in the keyboard section. That's where you write using a stylus. To use your finger to draw and write text, tap the handwriting icon (the blank rectangle) Ⓐ.

Ⓐ Changing the input method

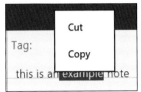

B Text handles

C Context menu

To work with text in touch mode:

When you're using the onscreen keyboard to type text, you can use your finger or stylus to highlight text on the screen or to access a context menu so you can do things like cut, copy, and paste.

1. Tap a tile app on the Start screen that requires typing, such as Mail, Bing, or Internet Explorer.

2. Tap a text box on the screen, and type something using the onscreen keyboard.

3. Tap a typed word. Handles appear around the word **B**. Drag the handles to highlight more or less text.

4. Tap and hold the highlighted word to access a context menu **C**.

To improve handwriting recognition:

1. Swipe in from the right edge of the screen, tap the Settings charm, and then tap the *PC Settings* link.

2. Tap the *General* link under Settings, and tap the *Language Preferences* link under Language.

3. Tap the *Options* link under Add a Language .

D Language options

4. To set handwriting as the default for writing with a stylus or your finger, tap the "Write characters in freehand" option under the Handwriting heading ⓔ. To write each character as a separate letter, tap the "Write each character separately" option.

5. Tap the *Personalize handwriting recognition* link ⓔ.

continues on next page

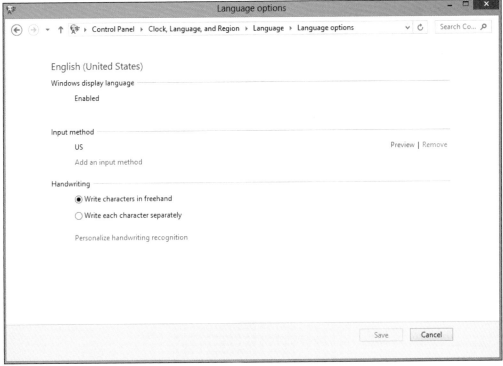

ⓔ Setting the writing style

6. Tap the *Target specific recognition errors* link 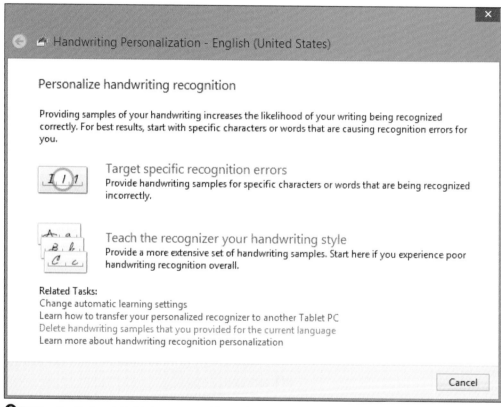.

or

Tap the *Teach the recognizer your handwriting style* link.

These two links will take you through a series of handwriting exercises designed to help train the Surface tablet to recognize your writing style.

TIP If you take the time to train the Surface tablet writing freehand on the tablet will be more enjoyable.

TIP You can change languages by tapping the *Advanced settings* link **D**.

TIP You can also change the language of the keyboard. If you have two keyboard languages installed and are using a physical keyboard, you can create a shortcut to switch between languages by tapping the *Advanced settings* link **D** and then tapping the *Change language bar hot keys* link. This is a feature designed more for Windows 8 than for the tablet.

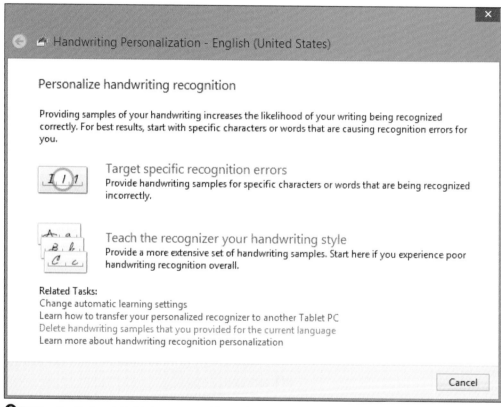

×

Handwriting Personalization - English (United States)

Personalize handwriting recognition

Providing samples of your handwriting increases the likelihood of your writing being recognized correctly. For best results, start with specific characters or words that are causing recognition errors for you.

Target specific recognition errors
Provide handwriting samples for specific characters or words that are being recognized incorrectly.

Teach the recognizer your handwriting style
Provide a more extensive set of handwriting samples. Start here if you experience poor handwriting recognition overall.

Related Tasks:
Change automatic learning settings
Learn how to transfer your personalized recognizer to another Tablet PC
Delete handwriting samples that you provided for the current language
Learn more about handwriting recognition personalization

Cancel

F Training the Surface tablet to learn your writing style

Mail and Outlook.com

The Mail, People, Calendar, and Messaging apps share account information. That means that if you enter your Gmail email account to add contacts to the People app, you will also be able to access the Gmail account in the Mail app. Of course, not all account information is shared across all apps. For example, the Messaging app doesn't access Gmail accounts, so you can't use the Messaging app on the tablet to have IM conversations with Gmail contacts. It can be a bit confusing, but the chapter for each app specifies supported accounts.

By visiting Outlook.com in a web browser, you can access information that allows you to do more with People, Mail, Calendar, Messaging, and SkyDrive. This chapter focuses on the Mail app and how it, along with People and Calendar, uses Outlook.com to do more on the tablet.

In This Chapter

Mail Accounts

You can use the Mail app to manage multiple email accounts. It handles basic email functions (such as attachments), saves drafts, and has some editing features.

To add a Microsoft account:

1. Tap the Mail tile on the Start screen.
2. On the Add Your Microsoft Account screen, enter your Microsoft email address and password. Tap Save.

   If you've already connected your Microsoft account to the People app, the mailbox for that email account appears when you open the Mail app **A**.

▸ **Mail accounts.** A list of email accounts displays in this panel. Any folders for the mailboxes of accounts connected to the Mail app appear here as well.

▸ **Email messages.** A list of email messages displays here. Tap a folder to see the emails in that folder.

▸ **Create an email.** Tap the plus (+) button to start a new email.

▸ **Sync.** Tap this button to refresh the mailbox.

▸ **Pin to Start.** Tap this button to pin an email account's tile to the Start screen.

Mail accounts   *Email messages*   *Create an email*

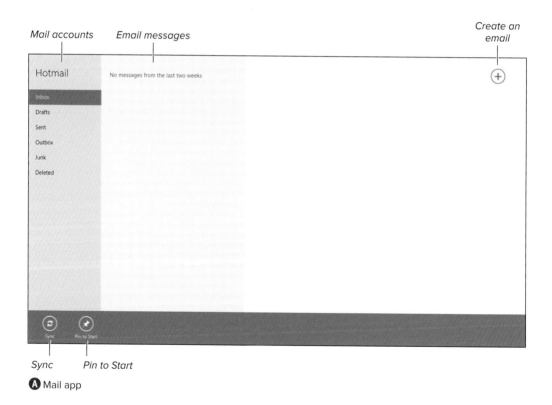

Sync   *Pin to Start*

A Mail app

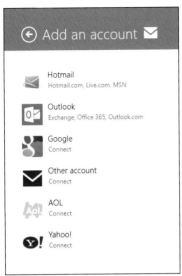

B Adding an email account

C Email accounts in the Mail app

To add another email account:

You can add additional email accounts to the mailbox so you can view all your email accounts in one app.

1. Swipe in from the right of the screen and tap the Settings charm. Tap Accounts, and tap the *Add an account* link **B**.

2. Tap an email account provider (Hotmail, Outlook, Google, AOL, Yahoo, or Other account).

3. On the Add Your [*Email Provider*] Account screen, enter the email address and password for the selected account in the text boxes.

4. Tap Connect. The Mail app syncs with the account and creates new folders in the Mail accounts panel **C**.

5. Tap the account to see messages and folders from that account.

To manage and remove email accounts:

1. Swipe in from the right edge of the screen, tap the Settings charm, and tap Accounts.

2. Tap the email account that you want to manage or remove (Hotmail, Outlook, Google, AOL, Yahoo, or Other). Options for that email account appear 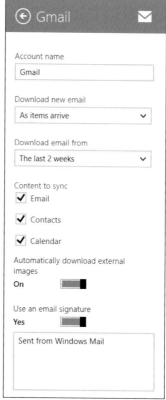. Flick up and down the panel to see more options.

   ▸ **Account name.** Tap the text box, tap the X in the corner to delete the current name, and type a new name. This name appears as the email account name in the Mail app.

   ▸ **Download new email.** Tap the down arrow to choose when new email should be downloaded: as items arrive, every 15 minutes, every 30 minutes, hourly, or manually.

   ▸ **Download email from.** Tap the down arrow to choose whether to download email from the last 3 days, the last 7 days, the last 2 weeks, the last month, or any time.

   ▸ **Content to sync.** Tap the check boxes to choose what type of content from this email account syncs with the Mail, People, and Calendar apps: Email, Contacts, and/or Calendar. Note that all apps won't be available for all email accounts.

D Managing email accounts

E Removing an email account

▸ **Automatically download external images.** Drag the slider to choose whether or not the Mail app should download external images for this email account automatically. Drag the slider to turn this option on or off.

▸ **Use an email signature.** Add a signature to your emails. Tap the text box and type a message that you want to appear at the end of all emails sent from this account on the Surface tablet. Drag the slider to turn the feature on or off.

▸ **Show Email notifications for this account.** Drag the slider to turn Start screen notifications of new emails on or off.

▸ **Remove account.** Tap the All My Synced PCs button to remove the account from all Microsoft devices that access this account. Tap the This PC button to remove the email account from the Surface tablet **E**.

TIP Email doesn't always send the minute you tap the Send button. If this happens, tap the Sync button and the message will be sent.

TIP Some email accounts might have additional settings, such as email server and port information, that can be found by scrolling down in the Email Account Settings panel.

TIP If an email account will work with other apps, such as People or Calendar, it will appear in the Account Settings panel.

TIP To turn grouping messages by conversation on or off, tap Options in the Settings charm.

Email

Even if you have a lot of email accounts in the Mail app, handling email from different accounts is straightforward. You can mark emails as unread or move them into folders already created within that email account. However, you can't use the Mail app to create new folders.

Working with email:

The upper-right corner of the email screen usually has three buttons **A**. If there aren't any emails in your inbox or in the email folder you're currently viewing, only the New Message (+) button appears.

- **New Message.** Tap this button to start a new email.

- **Respond.** Tap this button to display a context menu with the options Reply, Reply All, and Forward.

- **Delete.** Tap this button to delete an email. There is no option to confirm the delete. To recover the deleted email, tap the Deleted folder in the account's mailbox.

New Message

Respond

Delete

A Create and send email.

To create an email:

1. Tap the New Message (+) button in the message screen. A blank email screen appears **B**.

B Creating an email

2. Tap the down arrow next to your name, and tap the email account you want to use to send the email.

3. Tap the text box below To, and enter an email address. Tap the plus (+) button to add more recipients.

4. Tap the down arrow below Priority to change the priority setting.

5. Tap the Add a Subject box, and type a subject line.

6. Tap below the blue line in the message screen, and type a message.

7. Swipe up from the bottom of the screen to reveal the app bar and access the following options **C**:

   ▸ **Save draft.** Tap to save a draft of the email.

   ▸ **Attachments.** Tap to add an attachment, and choose the location of the attachment from the Files menu. Tap the attachment and tap the Attach button.

   ▸ **Copy/Paste.** Tap this button to copy or paste text.

   ▸ **Font.** Tap this button for a context menu where you can tap a standard font size (from 8 to 36 points) and a font style (Cambria, Calibri, Consolas, Arial, Times New Roman, Tahoma, Verdana, or Georgia). Flick up and down in the menu to see more options.

   ▸ **Bold.** To make text bold, select some text and tap this button; or tap this button before typing.

   ▸ **Italic.** To make text italic, select some text and tap this button; or tap this button before typing.

   ▸ **Underline.** To underline text, select some text and tap this button; or tap this button before typing.

   ▸ **Text color.** To change the color of text, tap this button to display a context menu and then tap a color: purple, magenta, white, purple, yellow, blue, orange, red, green, or gray. You can select a color before typing, or you can highlight some text and then select a color.

   ▸ **Emoticons.** Tap this button, and a plethora of emoticons appear on the right panel of the screen. Flick up and down the panel to see more options. Tap an emoticon and it appears at the position of the cursor in the email.

   ▸ **More.** Tap the More button for the formatting options Bulleted list, Numbered list, Undo, and Redo. Tap the format you want.

8. When you're finished composing the email, tap the Send button.

   or

   Tap the cancel button (it is the X in the upper-right corner of the message), and tap Save Draft to close it and return to it later.

   or

   Tap Delete Draft to delete the email.

C Email app bar

To move an email to a folder:

1. In the Messages list, tap the email you want to move.

2. Swipe up from the bottom of the screen to access the app bar, and tap the Move button. The entire screen fades to gray.

3. In the Mail accounts panel, tap the folder you want to move the email to. The email is moved. Note that you can move the email only to a folder within that email account.

To view email attachments:

You can save email attachments to folders on the Surface tablet.

1. Tap an email that has an attachment. The contents of the email appear in the message section of the screen.

2. Tap the Download button below the attachment **D**. An image of the file being downloaded appears.

3. Tap the image, and a context menu appears with the options Open, Open With, and Save **E**. Tap Open to view the file in an app that can open it. Tap Open With to select an app to open the file. Tap Save to save the attachment.

D Downloading an attachment

E Opening an attachment

To save an email attachment:

1. Tap an email that has an attachment, tap the attachment file, and tap Download.

2. Tap the attachment file image, and tap Save.

3. Save the file in the prompted location.

   or

   Tap a folder.

   or

   Tap the down arrow next to Files to choose another folder on the Surface tablet.

4. To give the attachment a new name, tap the text box, tap the X to delete the current file name, type a new file name, and tap Save 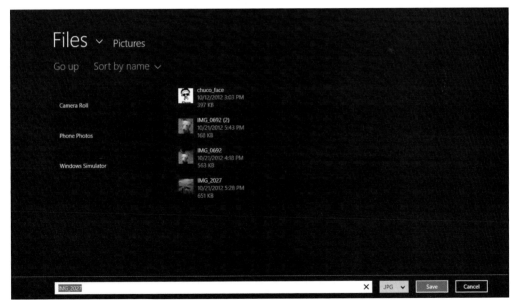.

TIP Changes made to the location of emails in an account on the Surface tablet are synced, and the changes appear wherever you access that email account.

TIP New folders created in connected web-based email accounts appear in the Mail app, but you can't create folders in the Mail app.

TIP When viewing a draft message, tap the icon that looks like a pencil to continue writing the email.

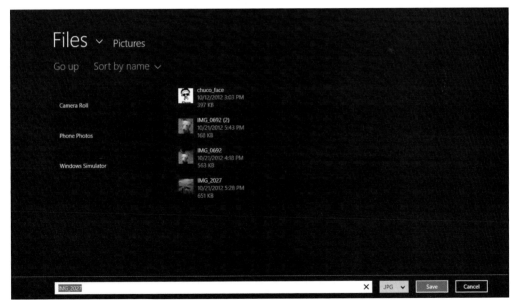

F Saving an attachment

Outlook.com

Microsoft has released a web-based version of Outlook that is essentially a hub that ties together Mail, People, Calendar, Messages, and SkyDrive. It's a cloud-based way to access information in all those accounts.

Although Outlook.com is not part of the Surface tablet, it is another way to interact with some of the apps on the Surface tablet when you're away from the tablet. This section includes working with People, Calendar, and Mail. SkyDrive and Messages are not included since Outlook.com doesn't add more functionality to them.

Changes made in Outlook.com to corresponding apps on the tablet will sync with the tablet. While you can manage your Microsoft email account using Oulook.com, it is very different from the traditional Outlook mail app. Since you will likely access the website from a computer, instructions in this section assume you're using a mouse.

 Quick view categories

 Accessing the Outlook.com navigation bar

 Shortcuts to Mail, People, Calendar, and SkyDrive

To access Outlook.com:

1. Open a web browser, type **Outlook.com**, and press Enter.

2. Type your Microsoft email account and password in the text boxes. Click the Sign In button.

   Your Microsoft email account inbox appears. (Note that none of the non-Microsoft email accounts that have been added to the Mail app will be shown here.) There are also quick views: These are predefined categories for emails that contain documents or photos, emails that are flagged, and emails that contain shipping updates; these can be used to quickly sort through emails in the mailbox.

3. Click a quick view to see emails related to that quick view category **A**. To create a new category, click New Category, enter a category name, and press Enter on the keyboard.

4. Click the down arrow next to Outlook **B** to see shortcuts to Mail, People, Calendar, and SkyDrive **C**.

To create a new Mail folder:

The first screen you see when entering Outlook.com is Mail. Tapping Mail in the navigation bar is just a shortcut back to this screen. Since you can't create new folders in the Mail app, you will need to create them in Outlook.com so they will appear in the Mail app on the tablet. If you don't see them immediately in the Mail app, tap the Sync button.

1. Click the *New folder* link at the bottom of the Folders heading, and type a name in the text box .

2. Press Enter on the keyboard. The new folder appears as the last folder in the list.

3. To move the folder to another folder in your email account, drag it to the folder and release.

D Creating a new Mail folder

To add contacts in Outlook.com:

Contacts that you add in Outlook.com will appear in the People app on the tablet. Accounts you have connected in the People app appear as icons in the upper-right corner of the screen.

1. Click the down arrow next to Outlook in the upper-left corner of the web page, and click People. A list of contacts in the People app appears in a column on the screen. You can search the list by typing a name in the search bar and clicking the Search icon .

E Searching for a contact

Add people to your contact list

f Facebook email addresses

g Google contacts

in LinkedIn contacts

←| Import from file

No, thanks

F Importing contacts from other accounts

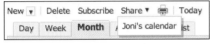

New ▾ Delete Subscribe Share ▾ 🖨 Today
Day Week **Month** Joni's calendar ist

G Calendars you can share

2. Add more contacts to the People app from Facebook, Google, LinkedIn, or an imported file. Click the Facebook, Google, LinkedIn, or Import from File icon **F**.

3. Click the Connect button. Enter your Microsoft email and password, and click the Sign In button.

4. Enter the email address and password associated with the account you're connecting to, and click either OK, I'll Allow It or Sign In (the options vary based on the account you're connecting). Your contacts sync with your People contacts.

To share a calendar:

One of the limitations of the Calendar app is that you can't share a calendar with others. To do that, you'll need to visit Outlook.com.

1. Click the down arrow next to Outlook in the upper-left corner of the web page, and click Calendar. A calendar view appears.

2. Click the *Share* link at the top of the calendar. Calendars associated with the Microsoft email account appear in a drop-down menu **G**.

3. Click the calendar you want to share.

continues on next page

4. Click the Share This Calendar option.

Options for how you want to share appear 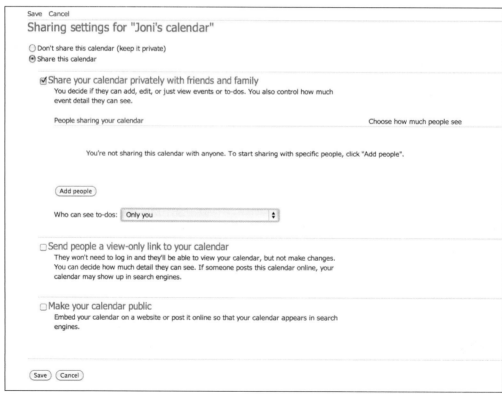.

5. Click the Add People button, and type the email address of the person you want to share the calendar with. You can also tap the Favorites tab to see contacts you've marked as favorites in the People app; click the box next to their name to share the calendar with them.

6. To choose calendar permissions for that person, click the View Details button. Click an option, and click the Add button.

7. Click the Save button on the Sharing Settings screen to send the invitation.

TIP Click the Keep Me Signed In check box to avoid having to enter your Microsoft email address and password every time you access Outlook.com from the same computer.

TIP To start an IM conversation in the People screen with any of your contacts online, follow the steps in "To start a chat from the Invite screen" in Chapter 6.

TIP To return to the main Outlook.com screen from the Calendar app, mouse over Windows Live and click Home in the upper-left corner of the web page.

Save   Cancel

Sharing settings for "Joni's calendar"

○ Don't share this calendar (keep it private)
◉ Share this calendar

☑ Share your calendar privately with friends and family
You decide if they can add, edit, or just view events or to-dos. You also control how much event detail they can see.

People sharing your calendar   Choose how much people see

You're not sharing this calendar with anyone. To start sharing with specific people, click "Add people".

(Add people)

Who can see to-dos: [Only you   ‡]

☐ Send people a view-only link to your calendar
They won't need to log in and they'll be able to view your calendar, but not make changes. You can decide how much detail they can see. If someone posts this calendar online, your calendar may show up in search engines.

☐ Make your calendar public
Embed your calendar on a website or post it online so that your calendar appears in search engines.

(Save) (Cancel)

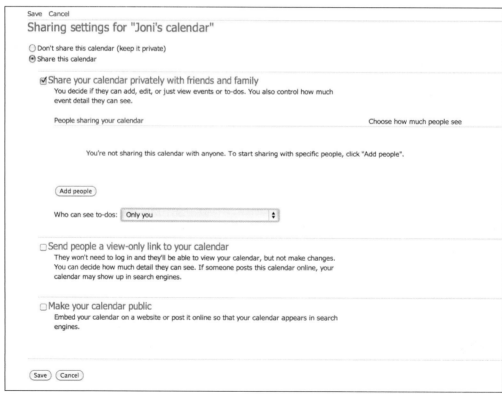 Sharing options

5

Calendar

The Calendar app is exactly what it sounds like: a calendar. There are multiple views available so you can display your information by the day, week, or month. Best of all, you can display a smaller version of Calendar in other apps, which makes planning easy.

Although Calendar seamlessly syncs calendars with any account in the tablet, you can't use the Calendar app to create or share calendars. That will need to be done through Outlook.com, which is accessible by launching Internet Explorer. (See Chapter 4, "Mail," for more information.)

In This Chapter

Calendar Views

The Calendar app is similar to other calendars, with month, week, and day views. The default view is the current month.

To change the Calendar view:

1. Tap the Calendar tile on the Start screen.

2. Swipe up from the bottom of the tablet to access the app bar **A**.

3. To view appointments for a specific day, tap Day. The day view displays two consecutive days (today and the previous day) **B**. Swipe left or right to switch days.

4. To view a week, swipe up from the bottom of the tablet and tap Week on the app bar **C**. Swipe left or right to view the next or previous week, respectively.

5. To view a month, swipe up from the bottom of the tablet and tap Month on the app bar **D**. Swipe left or right to view the next or previous month, respectively.

6. To see the current day in any Calendar view, swipe up from the bottom of the screen and tap Today on the app bar.

   or

   Press Ctrl+T on a keyboard.

To view, add, or edit Calendar in other apps:

1. If Calendar isn't already launched, tap the Calendar tile on the Start screen.

2. Press the Windows button on the tablet to return to the Start screen, and tap the app in which you want Calendar to appear.

A Calendar's app bar

B Day view

C Week view

D Month view

E Open app in the left panel

3. Swipe in from the left and snap Calendar to the divider bar.

4. Slowly drag the app you want toward the center of the screen until you see the divider bar, and then release **E**. Calendar displays beside the app.

5. Tap an appointment in Calendar to view or edit it **F**.

6. To add an appointment, swipe up in the Calendar panel and tap the plus (+) icon **G**.

TIP To move the Calendar panel to the right side of the screen, drag the small calendar icon from the left side to the right side of the screen and release when the divider bar appears.

F Editing a calendar appointment

G Adding an appointment

Calendar Appointments

Calendar displays appointments you enter as well as those you sync from an existing account. You can edit and share appointments. You can also mark them as private, but it only makes sense to do so on shared calendars.

To create an appointment from the month, week, or day view:

1. In the month, week, or day view, tap the day on which you want to create an appointment.

2. Type a name for the appointment Ⓐ.

3. Tap the message box under the appointment name on the right side of the screen to add more information.

Add a destination.

Select how often an appointment will occur.

Send appointment invitation

Set a reminder. Choose None, set a specific amount of time, or choose a time from 30 minutes to 2 hours before the event.

Close and save appointment

Delete appointment

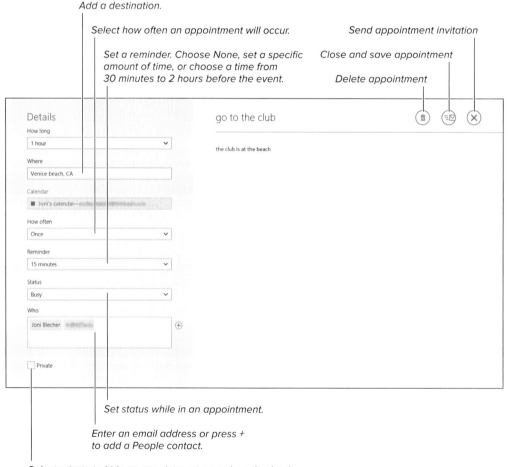

Set status while in an appointment.

Enter an email address or press + to add a People contact.

Select private to hide an appointment on a shared calendar or when adding comments you don't want anyone to see.

Ⓐ Appointment details

B Adding date and time details

4. In the Details section, tap the drop-down menus to make changes to the date, time, and duration. Enter text to describe the location, if desired **B**.

5. Tap the *Show more* link to add more details about the event **A**.

TIP Tap the plus (+) icon in the app bar to add an appointment from any view.

TIP Invite someone to an appointment by entering their email address in the Who box and tapping Send.

Calendar Charms

The Charms bar in Calendar allows you to share information from an appointment, add accounts that have calendars associated with them, and customize how calendars appear.

To use Calendar's Share charm:

1. Tap Appointment in Calendar.

2. Highlight the content you want to share in the message 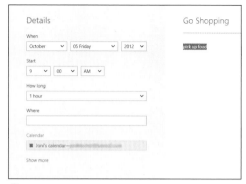 **A**.

3. Swipe in from the right edge of the tablet to display the Charms bar.

4. Tap Share **B**. Email options appear.

5. Tap the application you want to use to share the highlighted content.

6. Enter additional information in the Details screen, and tap Send **C**. The recipient will receive the information as an email, not as a Calendar appointment attachment.

A Highlight the content you want to share.

B Email options

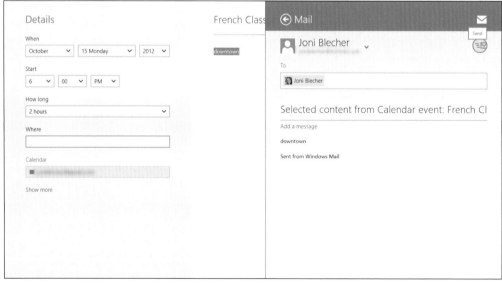

C Sending information from a Calendar appointment

To add accounts using the Settings charm:

1. Swipe in from the right edge, tap Settings in the Charms bar, and tap Accounts **D**.

2. Tap the *Add an account* link **E**.

3. In the right pane, tap the type of account you want to add **F**.

4. Enter your email address and password, and tap Connect **G**. If there's a calendar associated with that email account, the appointments will populate the Calendar app.

D Account settings

E Adding an account

F Selecting an account type

G Entering account information

To customize the Calendar view using the Settings charm:

1. Tap a Calendar view.

2. Swipe in from the right edge, tap Settings in the Charms bar, and tap Options **H**.

3. To change the color of a calendar, tap its drop-down menu in the Options pane and tap a color **I**.

4. To hide a calendar, slide its bar from right to left **J**.

TIP You can share a calendar with others in Outlook.com.

H Setting options in Settings

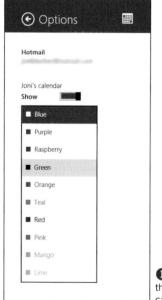

I Changing the color of a calendar

J Hiding a calendar

6

Messaging

Messaging is the instant messaging (IM) application for the Surface tablet. Think of it as Windows Live Messenger but with the ability to chat with people through Facebook. As of this writing, other IM clients—such as AOL, Google Talk, or Yahoo—are not supported, so you'll only be using Messaging for Facebook chats or Windows Live Messenger.

Although the look and feel is similar to the Messaging app on Windows Phone, there are some differences. Most notably, you can't use Messaging to send text messages or multimedia messages. The app supports threading, so you can view an entire IM session.

Messaging Accounts

When you open Messaging, you're alerted that you have been automatically signed in to your Microsoft account so that you can start chatting with other friends using the Messaging app. As of this writing, the only social media option is to add a Facebook account.

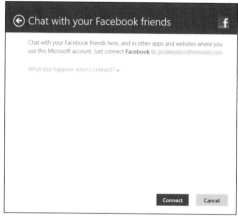

A Adding Facebook friends

To add a Facebook account:

1. Tap the Messaging tile on the Start screen.

2. Tap Facebook Friends to connect your Facebook account to Messaging **A**.

   If you've already connected your Facebook account to the People app, the small Facebook icon appears in the upper-right corner of the screen.

3. Tap Connect **B**, and the Facebook log-in window appears.

4. Enter your Facebook log-in information **C**, including email or phone and password; tap Log In.

TIP To manage your Facebook account settings, tap Accounts in the Settings charm.

B Connecting to Facebook

C Entering Facebook account information

A Messaging app bar

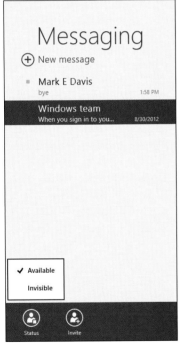

B Setting your status

Using Messaging

The Messaging app works similarly to the Windows Live Messenger app. You can set your message availability status, invite people to chat, and conduct IM sessions. It also saves all IM threads so you can go back and review them at any time.

To set your status:

1. With the Messaging app open, swipe up from the bottom of the tablet to display the app bar **A**.

2. Tap Status in the app bar.

3. Tap Available or Invisible in the Status pop-up menu **B**.

To start a chat:

1. In the Messaging app, tap the *New message* link to open the People app, where you can find someone to send a message to.

2. On the People screen, tap the *Online only* link and select a contact **C** (only people who are online via Facebook and Windows Live appear).

3. Tap Choose. A new message begins for the selected contact **D**.

4. Type a message in the text box, and tap Enter on the keyboard to send the message.

To invite new friends to chat:

1. Swipe up from the bottom edge of the tablet to display the app bar **E**.

2. Tap Invite. The People screen displays.

3. Enter the email address for the contact you want to invite to chat **F**, and tap Next.

4. Tap Invite.

C Choosing a contact who's currently online

D The Messaging chat window

E Inviting people to chat

F Adding a contact's email address

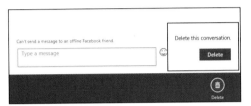

G Finding
contacts online

H Creating a
chat message

I Deleting a conversation thread

J A message notification

To start a chat from the Invite screen:

1. Tap the messaging icon on the upper-right corner of the screen that launched when you tapped Invite.

2. Tap the box under "Messaging," and type the name of the person you want to chat with; possible matches appear as you type. Tap the name of the person you want to chat with **G**.

   or

   Tap an existing IM thread in the People screen.

3. Type a message in the text box at the lower-right corner of the screen, and tap Return **H**.

To view or delete a completed chat:

1. Tap the message thread that you want to view.

2. Swipe up from the bottom of the tablet to display the app bar.

3. To delete the thread, tap Delete, and then tap Delete again in the pop-up to confirm the action **I**.

To access a message from a notification:

Tap the notification **J** to return to the Messaging app and display the conversation window.

> **TIP** The option "Add People to Your Contact List from Networks like Facebook, LinkedIn, Twitter and Others" just imports those contacts to People. If you connect Google, for example, you're importing contacts, not adding the ability to use Google Chat from the Messaging app.

> **TIP** Facebook chats performed using the Messaging app will also be saved on Facebook.

Messaging Snapped Mode

You can view Messaging even while you're using other apps.

To view Messaging messages in other apps:

1. If Messaging isn't already running, tap the Messaging tile on the Start screen.

2. Press the Windows button on the tablet to return to the Start screen, and tap the app you want to have Messaging appear in.

3. Swipe in from the left to reveal the left-side panel .

A Open apps

4. Slowly drag Messaging toward the center of the screen until you see the divider bar, and then release **Ⓑ**.

5. Tap a conversation in Messaging to view or continue it.

6. Swipe up in the Messaging panel to display the app bar so you can set your status or invite people to chat **Ⓒ**.

> **TIP** When you're not using the Messaging app, new messages will appear as notifications in the upper-right corner of the screen.

Ⓑ Displaying Messaging in the split screen

Ⓒ Messaging's app bar menu

Messaging Charms

The only charm that works with the Messaging app is the Settings charm. Use it to add or remove accounts and to turn on or off the ability to send messages.

To remove an account from Messaging:

1. Swipe in from the right edge of the screen to access the Charms bar.
2. Tap Settings, and then tap Accounts.
3. Tap the account you'd like to remove .
4. Tap the *Manage this account online* link **B**.
5. Tap the *Remove this connection completely* link.
6. Tap Remove **C**.

To turn on or off the ability to send messages:

1. Swipe in from the right edge of the screen to access the Charms bar.
2. Tap Settings, and then tap Options.
3. Slide the bar to the left to turn off messages; slide the bar right to turn messages on **D**.

A Facebook settings

B Accessing your Facebook account

C Removing a Facebook account

D Turning messages on or of

7

People

After the initial tablet setup, the best place to start entering information is in the People app, which is where information about your contacts is stored. Once People is populated, working with related apps such as Mail, Messaging, and Calendar will be a breeze. The People tile on the Start screen will populate automatically with cycling pictures associated with your contacts.

People goes beyond contacts that might be stored in a phonebook or in the address book integrated into Microsoft Outlook. People serves as a one-stop shop for all the people you know from all the places you know them, and it brings contacts that live online or in an existing Microsoft Exchange account into one place. This includes social media sites such as Facebook, Twitter, and LinkedIn.

Keeping all the people you know in one place makes it easy to see what's going on with them across multiple locations.

In This Chapter

Adding Accounts

There are a couple of ways to add contacts to People. If you have a lot of contacts already stored in different accounts online, then just add those accounts to People. However, not all online accounts are represented in the Settings options for People; for example, there isn't an option for AOL or Yahoo accounts.

To open People's Settings options:

1. Tap the People tile on the Start screen. As is the case with other applications on the Surface tablet, you'll need to access the Charms bar to make changes.

2. To make the Charms bar appear, swipe from the right edge of the tablet **A**.

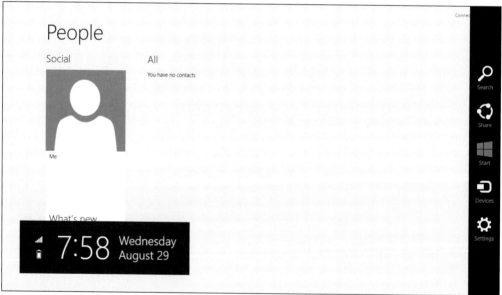

A The People screen with the Charms bar

B Settings menu

C Accounts that can be added to People

3. Tap Settings. The Settings menu appears **B**.

   If you have a keyboard attached, you can access Settings by pressing **⊞**+I.

To add an existing email account to People:

1. In People's Settings screen, tap Accounts **B**. A new screen appears, listing all accounts. Whichever Microsoft account (Hotmail, Live, Outlook.com, or MSN) you signed in with when setting up the tablet should already be listed.

2. Select Add an Account to see the list of online accounts that can be added **C**.

3. Tap the account you want to add.

4. Enter your email address and password for the selected account **D**. The tablet syncs with your account and imports your contacts.

   Note that the tablet needs to be connected to the Internet for this to work. When syncing is finished, contacts begin to populate the screen.

   Use the same process to add additional email accounts.

D A similar setup bar appears for each account you add.

To add a social media account to People:

1. On People's Settings screen **B**, tap Accounts. A screen appears, listing all accounts you've already signed in with.

2. Select Add an Account to see the list of online accounts that can be added. Social networking sites such as Facebook, Twitter, and LinkedIn are listed **C**.

3. Tap the type of account you want to add. You are prompted to allow your main Microsoft account (Hotmail, MSN, Outlook.com, or Live) to access that account.

4. Tap Connect.

5. Enter your login and password, and tap Authorize App **E**. The tablet syncs with your account and imports your contacts.

Note that the tablet needs to be connected to the Internet for this to work. When syncing is finished, contacts begin to populate the screen.

Use the same process to set up additional social media accounts.

TIP When you enter an email address using the onscreen keyboard **D**, note that there are dedicated @ and .com keys.

TIP One of the benefits of connecting your social media accounts is that you will be able to easily update your status and share links, photos, and documents directly from the People application.

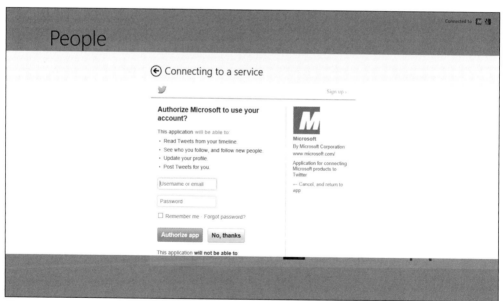

E Authorize Microsoft to use your account.

Adding and Editing Contacts

If you don't want to populate People with tons of contacts from multiple accounts, you can add one contact at a time. Swipe from the bottom edge of the tablet to make the app bar appear Ⓐ. You can also access the app bar by pressing ⊞+Z.

The app bar contains three options:

- **Home** makes the app bar disappear; it will not take you back to the Start screen.

- **Online Only** shows contacts who are online, making it easier to start virtual conversations.

- **New** is for adding contacts.

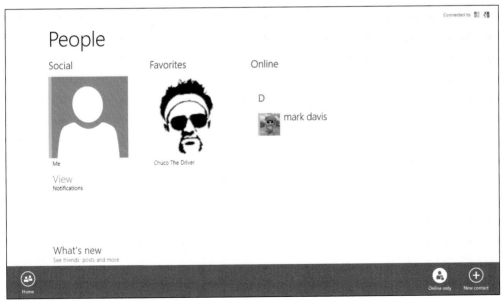

Ⓐ The app bar in People

To create a contact in People:

1. Tap New on the app bar at the bottom of the People app. The New Contact screen **B** launches.

2. In the Account drop-down menu, select the account that you want to save the new contact to.

3. Fill out the information for the new contact. You can enter three email addresses (personal, other, and work), up to nine phone numbers (a pager, and two each for mobile, home, work, and fax), three addresses, and information such as job title, significant other, website, and notes.

4. When you are finished adding the contact information, tap Save in the lower-right corner of the screen.

Add up to three addresses.

Other options include website, job title, significant other, and notes.

New contact

Account

Hotmail

Name
First name

Last name

Company

(+) Name

Email
Personal

(+) Email

Phone
Mobile

(+) Phone

Address
(+) Address

Other info
(+) Other info

Save   Cancel

Add up to nine phone numbers.

Tap Save to complete.

B Contact card

C Searching for contacts in People

D Favoriting a contact

E Linking information for a contact

To edit a contact in People:

1. Swipe from the right edge to access the Charms bar, tap Search, enter the name of the contact you'd like to edit, and tap their name in the search results **C**. The name card for the selected contact appears.

2. Swipe from the bottom of the screen to make the app bar appear.

3. Tap an option on the app bar at the bottom of the display:

   ▶ **Pin to Start.** Select this if you want to "pin" this contact to the Start screen and make the contact a tile.

   ▶ **Favorite.** The contact will appear on the People start screen, making it easy to see their updates and contact information. Tap the Favorite button (it has a star on it) to mark someone as a Favorite contact **D**.

   ▶ **Link.** Select this if you have a contact entered in multiple accounts. Say, for example, you have contact information for ABC News in two different accounts—tap the Link button to link the two contact cards together into one card **E**.

   ▶ **Edit.** This option allows you to make changes to the contact information, such as address, name, phone number, and email.

TIP To find a contact quickly, select Search from the Charms bar and type their name.

TIP Favorite contacts are usually those with whom you interact most often or those for whom you want to see updates.

Viewing Contacts

Once information about a particular contact has been entered, the card becomes dynamic, and you can do more with it. For example, ABC News 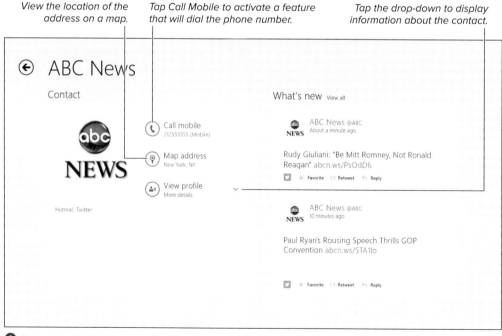 started as a contact from Twitter, and it has been edited to include additional information, such as a phone number and a website. At a glance, the contact card shows basic information and the latest tweets from ABC News.

You have several options on this card now that it has information entered.

- **Call Mobile.** Selecting this prompts an application that dials the number attached to the contact. If a phone application isn't loaded, you will be prompted to look for one in the Microsoft Store.

View the location of the address on a map. *Tap Call Mobile to activate a feature that will dial the phone number.* *Tap the drop-down to display information about the contact.*

ⓐ Contact card in People

- **Map Address.** This appears if an address or general location (city, state) is associated with the contact. Select this, and Maps launches to show the address, city, or state on a map.

- **View Profile.** Choose More Details from the drop-down menu to see all the information the contact card has to offer **B**. The information is dynamic. For example, if there's a website, tap the URL and there's an option to copy it or open the link.

When you're finished viewing contact information, tap the back arrow until you return to the People start screen, or pull up the app bar from the bottom of the screen and tap Home.

As you add more and more accounts to People, you may notice that the contacts are getting a bit crowded. Sure, you may follow hundreds of people on Twitter and have tons of Facebook friends, but that doesn't mean you want to see them every time you open the People application.

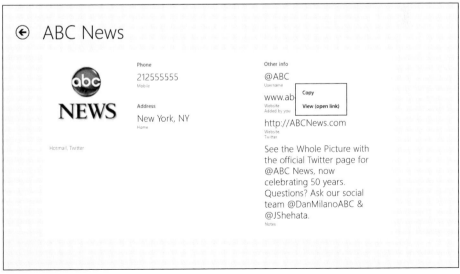

B Contact details

To manage the People view:

1. Choose Settings from the Charms bar. (To access the Charms bar, swipe from the right edge of the screen or press ⊞+I.)

2. On the Settings screen, tap Options. Contacts can be displayed by last name or first name **C**. Technically, the only choice is to turn on sorting contacts by last name. If you turn that off, then it will sort contacts by first name.

3. To limit the number of accounts that are displayed in People, select the check box next to the account you want displayed. For example, if you want to see only Gmail contacts, select the Gmail check box and leave the others unselected.

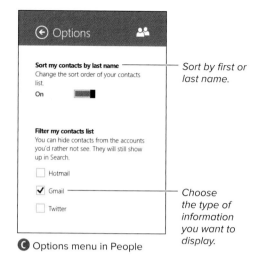

Sort by first or last name.

Choose the type of information you want to display.

C Options menu in People

If you don't want to see all the information about the people you know, you can just view the letters of the alphabet, which correspond to the contacts listed in the People app. So if you're looking for Tina York, you can select "T" or "Y" (depending on how you organized your contacts) to narrow down your search. To access this menu, tap the small horizontal line in the lower-right corner of the People start screen 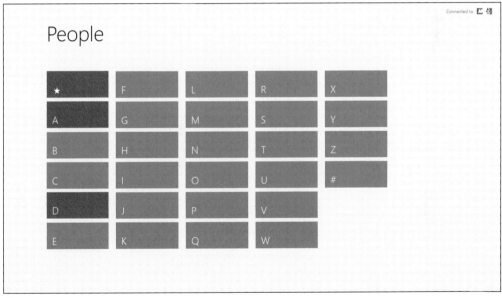. You can also access it via semantic zoom, which is achieved by making the "pinch" gesture on the screen.

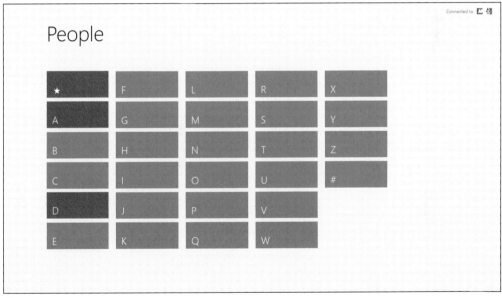

D Contacts by alphabet

Sharing Contacts

Once contacts have been added to People, you can share them. Find a contact that you want to share, and then select Share from the Charms bar. (Access the Charms bar by swiping from the right edge of the tablet.) The Share panel will show you how the contact information can be shared. In this example, the only option is to send the contact details via Mail.

To share contacts:

1. Select Mail in the People's Share menu.

   As the Mail application launches, the right panel widens and occupies almost half of the tablet screen **A**. A Mail message appears, with the contact card already inserted in the body of the text.

2. To change the email account the message will be sent from, tap the down arrow to the right of your name and then tap the account you want to use **B**.

3. In the To box, enter the email address of the person you want to send the contact card to.

4. To add a note to the message, tap in the message box. The cursor appears and you can start typing **C**.

5. To send the message, tap the button that looks like a circle with an envelope in it.

> **TIP** If the person you are sending the message to is already in your contacts, just start typing the first few letters of their name, and their email address will appear. Select the one you want to use by tapping it.

> **TIP** The keyboard shortcut to access the Share charm is ⊞+H.

A Sharing contact information

B Locating an email address

C Enter text in the message box.

A Deleting a contact

Deleting Contacts

There are two options for deleting contacts. You can delete an individual contact or an entire account.

To delete an individual contact from People:

1. Select the contact you want to delete.
2. Swipe from the bottom to reveal the app bar.
3. Tap Delete, and an option to delete the contact appears **A**.
4. Tap the Delete button to delete the contact.

To delete an email account from People:

1. Select Settings from the Charms bar, and tap Accounts **B**. The email accounts you have entered appear.
2. Tap the account you want to delete.
3. Tap the Remove Account button **C**.

   Note that If you choose to remove your primary Microsoft account, it will remove all accounts.

B Accounts option in Settings

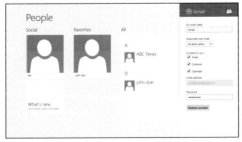

C Removing an account

To delete a social media account from People:

1. Select Settings from the Charms bar, and tap Accounts. The social media accounts you have entered appear **D**.

2. Tap the account you want to delete.

3. Tap Manage This Account Online **E**.

   Note that you will need to be connected to the Internet to remove the account or make adjustments in the settings.

4. To remove the account, tap the *Remove This Connection Completely* link **F**.

TIP If you don't want to delete an account completely, you can modify how it interacts with your Microsoft account.

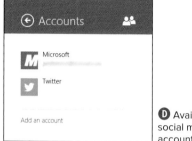

D Available social media accounts

E Social media account details

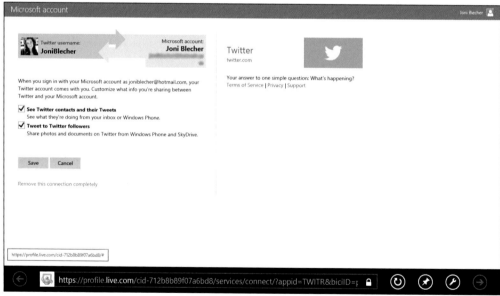

F Removing a Twitter account

Bing and Internet Explorer

Although you can use Bing and Internet Explorer (IE) to get online, they are two separate apps on the Windows RT Surface tablet. IE10 offers a full web experience. IE10 is where you'll store bookmarks, and it's what delivers everything else you might expect from a web browser.

Bing is what you'll use to search the web. Search results are provided in a graphical user interface. Tapping a selection launches Internet Explorer and delivers a full web experience. Bing has some fun features, such as hotspots that provide a little more information about the image on the screen. Bing also powers the Maps app.

In This Chapter

Bing

Bing doesn't have an app bar. It's simply a search engine app, and everything you need to know about it can be found on the Bing home screen.

To use the Bing home screen:

1. Tap the Bing tile on the Start screen.

2. Tap a square on the screen to activate a hotspot . This provides information about a detail on the screen **B**. Tap the colored text links to see search results for the hotspots.

3. Tap the "i" icon in the lower-left of the screen for information about the image **C**.

A Bing hotspots

B Hotspot detail

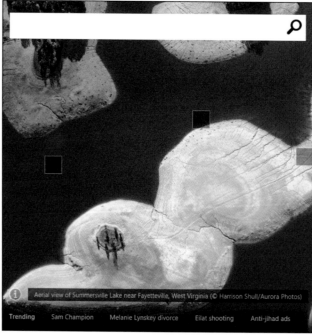

C Image information

D Trending topics

E Trending topic stories

To use Bing Trending:

Trending is a way to keep you updated on what's popular on the Internet. Think of it as "what everyone is talking about." At the bottom of the Bing home screen are currently trending topics.

1. Tap the *Trending* link at the bottom of the Bing home screen to see stories about trending topics **D**. Tap any link to see stories and images about that topic.

   Trending topics display as tiles **E**.

2. Tap a story to launch IE and display the story's website.

To search with Bing:

Bing's primary purpose on the Surface tablet is to be an Internet search engine.

1. Tap the search box on the Bing home screen, and type a query **F**. Search results appear on the screen as you type **F**. (To delete the search text, tap the X on the right side of the search box.)

2. Tap a result, and its website displays.

continues on next page

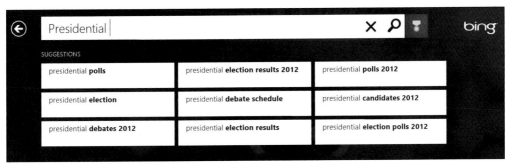

F Typing a search query

3. Tap Images to see pictures related to the search **G**.

4. Tap an image to enlarge it and see information about the website it comes from **H**. Flick right to left to scroll through images. Tap the back arrow (to the left of the search bar) to go back to the previous screen.

TIP Even if Bing doesn't display a list of possibilities for your search criteria on the Bing home screen, tap the Search icon and you'll still get results.

TIP Tap the Bing logo to return to the Bing home screen.

TIP Tap the *More* link in the lower-right corner of the Bing home screen to see more trending topics.

G Search-related images

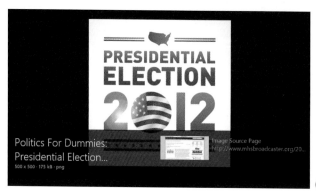

H Image source

 Search charm

 Share charm

Bing Charms

You can use charms with Bing to search, share search results, send results to other devices, and set permissions.

To use the Search charm:

1. Swipe in from the right edge to reveal the Charms bar, tap Search, and enter a search query **A**. Possible search matches appear. If you see one that fits, tap it.

   You can search something other than Bing.

2. In the Search charm, tap the icon of the app you want to search in, and then tap the Search icon.

To use the Share charm:

You can share search results with social media sites via People or email.

1. Swipe in from the right edge to display the Charms bar, tap Share, and then tap People or Mail **B**.

2. If you tapped People in step 1, skip to step 3. If you tapped Mail, type an email address in the To box. Tap the *Add a message* link, type a message, and tap the Send button. You can skip the following steps.

continues on next page

3. Tap the down arrow next to Facebook. Social media sites that you're connected to and that can share information from Bing appear. Tap the social media site you want to post the link on. Tap the *Add a message* link to say something about the post **C**.

4. Tap the Send button to post to the social media site.

C Sharing search results on your Facebook wall

To use the Devices charm:

You can send search results to other devices that are connected to your Surface tablet.

1. Swipe in from the right edge to reveal the Charms bar, and tap Devices to see available devices (such as Printer or Second Screen) **D**.

2. Tap a device to connect. Second Screen is a way to extend what's on the tablet's display to other screens, such as monitors and TVs. If you tap Second Screen, there will be options for PC Screen Only, Duplicate, Extend, and Second Screen Only. If you tap Printer, tap the Print button.

D Devices charm

To connect accounts to Bing:

1. Swipe in from the right edge to display the Charms bar, tap Settings, and then tap Accounts.

   Facebook and your Microsoft account can connect with Bing.

2. To connect those accounts with Bing, tap the Sign In button.

3. Tap the password box on the Connecting to a Service screen, and enter the email address and password for the account.

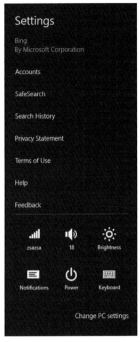

E Settings charm

F SafeSearch settings

To choose SafeSearch settings:

The Settings charm in Bing allows you to choose settings for your protection. Use it to set up parameters for search results and to manage your search history.

1. Swipe in from the right edge of the screen to display the Charms bar, tap Settings, and then tap SafeSearch **E**.

    The SafeSearch charm contains options for filtering adult content **F**.

    ▸ **Strict.** Filters out any possible adult content.

    ▸ **Moderate.** Filters only adult images and videos from search results.

    ▸ **Off.** There's no filter; anything can come up in the search results.

2. Tap a filter to control the type of search results you want.

To set search history settings:

1. Swipe in from the right edge to display the Charms bar, tap Settings, and then tap Search History **E**.

2. Drag the slider to On to keep a history of your Bing searches **G**.

3. Tap Clear All to erase your search history **G**.

G Managing Bing's search history

TIP The Share panel will show all the apps that can be used to share Internet links.

TIP If you choose to connect your Facebook account to Bing, the app will have access to posts in your news feed.

TIP Bing has a rewards program. Sign up for the program to receive credits for searching with Bing and taking part in special offers.

TIP Parents can select the Strict setting in SafeSearch if they don't want their children to get racy results.

Internet Explorer

IE is the web browser for the Surface tablet. It works similarly to the way the browser works on the Desktop, however there are a few noteworthy design changes; for example, the URL bar is at the bottom of the screen instead of at the top.

If this is your first time using Internet Explorer, the MSN site will appear on the screen. If not, the last site you visited displays.

The app bar appears at the bottom of the screen **A**.

Here's what you can do with the IE app bar:

- **Go back.** Tap this to go back to the previous web page you were viewing.

- **URL bar.** Type in a new URL or tap in the URL box to reveal frequently visited sites or favorites.

- **Refresh.** Reloads the website.

- **Pin to Start / Add to Favorites.** Tap Pin to Start to save a site as a tile on the Start screen (this is known as *pinning*). Tap Add to Favorites to save a website as a favorite; think of it as a bookmark.

- **Find on Page / View on Desktop.** Tap Find on Page, and type a word you want to find on the website. If you prefer the traditional IE view, tap View on Desktop to launch it in the Desktop.

- **Go Forward.** Tap this to go forward in your browser history. This works only if you've visited multiple websites and have navigated back to a previous site.

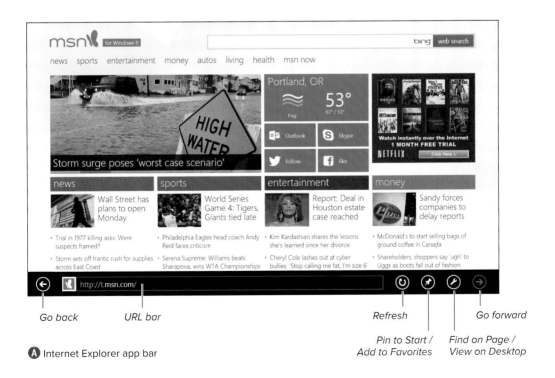

Go back   URL bar   Refresh   Go forward

                          Pin to Start /   Find on Page /
                          Add to Favorites View on Desktop

A Internet Explorer app bar

If there's a website that you visit often, save it as a tile on the Start screen so you won't have to launch IE and search for it or enter the URL to visit it. You can also save a site as a favorite so it appears in the dock of websites that display when you tap the URL bar.

There is a top app bar in IE, and it functions essentially as tabs. Use it to see websites that are running, open new windows, or open an InPrivate window. InPrivate is a way to view websites without having any history about them saved.

To display or hide the IE app bars:

1. Tap the IE tile on the Start screen. To reveal the app bar, swipe up from the bottom of the screen or down from the top of the screen.

2. To hide the app bar, tap anywhere on the screen.

   or

   To hide the bottom app bar, swipe down from the top of the app bar.

To use the URL bar in IE:

You can use the URL bar to view frequently visited sites, access favorite websites, enter URLs for websites, or copy or paste a URL.

1. Swipe up from the bottom of the IE screen to display the app bar.

2. Tap in the URL bar **B**. The Frequent and Favorites websites display in the dock.

3. Tap the tile of the site you want to visit **C**.

4. Swipe down from the top of the app bar to hide it. Swipe up from the bottom of the IE screen to make the app bar reappear.

5. Swipe from right to left on the horizontal scroll bar to see tiles for the websites in the Favorites dock **D**.

continues on next page

B URL bar in IE

C Displaying frequently visited websites

D Displaying the Favorites dock

6. Tap a Favorites tile to visit that site  **E**.

7. To visit a new URL, tap the URL bar to highlight the existing URL. When the onscreen keyboard appears, type the new URL. Popular URLs appear as options as you type. If the URL you want to visit appears as an option, tap its tile **F**. If it doesn't appear, then keep typing the URL and tap Go on the keyboard.

8. Highlight the URL, and tap and hold to display the options to cut or copy the URL **G**.

To pin a website to the Start screen:

1. Visit a site you'd like to pin to the Start screen, and swipe up from the bottom to display the IE app bar.

2. Tap the pin icon **H**.

3. Tap the Pin to Start option. The URL and the tile for the website display in a pop-up.

4. Tap the Pin to Start button **I**.

E Launching a Favorites site

F Tiles that match the URL text display as results.

G Selecting the option to cut or copy a URL

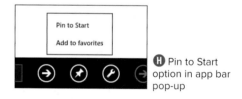

H Pin to Start option in app bar pop-up

I Saving a website as a tile on the Start screen

Start

J A website tile pinned to the Start screen

5. Tap the Windows key on the tablet to return to the Start screen. The new tile displays on the Start screen **J**.

   Once you've pinned a site, it appears in the dock of websites that display when you tap the URL bar.

6. Tap and hold the pinned website in the dock, and release when you see a context menu. Tap Open in New Tab, or tap Remove to delete it from the Start screen.

To add a website to Favorites:

1. Visit a site you want to designate as a favorite, and swipe up from the bottom to display the app bar.

2. Tap the pin icon **H**.

3. Tap Add to Favorites **H**.

   Once you have added a site to Favorites, it appears in the dock of websites that display when you tap the URL bar **K**.

continues on next page

Pinned   Frequent   Favorites

Welcome to Flickr   MSN for   MSN for   CNN.com -
- Photo Sharing   Windows 8   Windows 8   Bing   Breaking News...
                                                   Belgrave House -   Bing
                                                   ebooks

http://www.cnn.com/   × →

K Website saved as a favorite

4. Tap and hold the website tile in the dock, and release when you see a context menu. Tap Open in New Tab, or tap Remove to delete it from the Start screen .

① The Open in New Tab and Remove options

To use tabs in IE:

1. Swipe down from the top of the screen to see tabs for open websites **⑩**.

2. Tap a tab to open the website, or tap X to close it **⑩**.

3. Tap the plus (+) icon in the upper-right corner of the screen to open a new tab. A blank URL bar and the dock appear on the screen.

4. Tap the URL bar, type a URL, and then tap the right arrow or tap Go on the onscreen keyboard. You can also select a tile from the Pinned, Frequent, or Favorites lists.

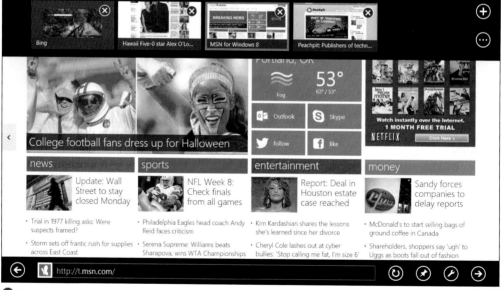

⑩ Open tabs

New InPrivate tab

Close tabs

N More tab options

New InPrivate tab

Close tabs

O Option to close tabs

InPrivate is turned on

P InPrivate mode

Turn on flip ahead   Close

Q Flipping ahead to the next page of a website

5. Tap the button with the three dots on the top app bar (these are tab tools) to display options to do more with tabs **N**.

6. Tap Close Tabs **O** to close all open tabs except the website you're currently viewing, which still appears as a tab.

7. To have a private IE experience, tap the button with the three dots in the top app bar and then tap InPrivate **P**. When this feature is on, IE won't save cookies, history, or other data about the websites you visit.

8. Tap the Turn on Flip Ahead button **Q**, and swipe from right to left to see the next page of the website you're viewing.

TIP If you're viewing IE on the Desktop, press the star icon in the upper-right corner of the screen to see Favorites sites.

TIP To change the name of a website you're about to pin, tap the text box in the pop-up that displays when you select Pin to Start and type a new name.

TIP A newly pinned tile may appear as the last tile on the Start screen. If you don't like where it initially appears, drag it to a new position on the Start screen.

IE Charms

You can use charms with IE to search, share search results, send results to other devices, and set permissions and Internet options.

To use the Search charm:

1. Swipe in from the right edge to display the Charms bar, tap Search, and enter a query in the search box **Ⓐ**. Possible search matches appear in a browser powered by Bing **Ⓑ**. If you see one that fits, tap it.

   You can search something other than Bing.

2. In the Search charm, tap the icon of the app you want to search in, and tap the Search icon. The app you want to search in appears on the screen **Ⓒ**.

Ⓐ Bing's Search charm

Ⓑ Search results powered by Bing

Ⓒ Searching in another app

① Share charm

③ Sharing the site on your Facebook wall

⑤ Devices charm

To use the Share charm:

You can share search results with social media sites via People or email. This section shows you how to share via social media. To share a link via email, see the "Bing Charms" section, earlier in this chapter.

1. Swipe in from the right edge to display the Charms bar, tap Share, and then tap People **①**.

2. Tap the down arrow next to Facebook, and social media sites that you're connected to and that can share information from IE appear. Tap the social media site you want to post the link on. Tap the *Add a message* link to say something about the post **③**.

3. Tap the Send icon to post to the selected social media site.

To use the Devices charm:

You can send websites to other devices that are connected to your Surface tablet.

1. Swipe in from the right edge to display the Charms bar, tap Devices, and tap Second Screen or Printer **⑤**. (Second Screen is a way to extend what's on the tablet's display to other screens, such as monitors and TVs.)

2. Tap a device to connect. Second Screen will have options for PC Screen Only, Duplicate, Extend, and Second Screen Only.

To use the Settings charm:

The Settings charm in IE is for fine-tuning IE settings. Use it to delete browser history, set location, manage zoom, set notifications, and use the flip ahead feature.

1. Swipe in from the right edge to display the Charms bar, tap Settings **G**, and tap Internet Options **H**.

   In the IE Settings, you can manage the IE options for history, location, zooming, and flipping ahead.

G IE Settings charm

H Internet Explorer settings

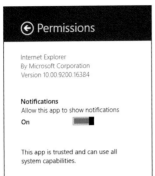

Internet Explorer
By Microsoft Corporation
Version 10.00.9200.16384

Notifications
Allow this app to show notifications
On

This app is trusted and can use all system capabilities.

❶ Setting Permissions

2. Swipe in from the right edge to display the Charms bar, tap Settings, and tap Permissions **❶**.

   Notifications appear on the Start screen when there is an update in the app.

3. Drag the Notifications slider on or off **❶**. Turn this feature off if you don't want to receive notifications on the Start screen.

TIP There are encoding options available in the Internet Explorer settings that are accessed via the Settings panel. If a webpage doesn't look correct, the encoding options may help.

TIP Opening Bing as a webpage in IE provides an additional setting in the IE app bar that you can use to switch to the Bing app.

9

Tile-Based Apps

The Surface tablet comes pre-populated with tile-based apps that are designed to keep you connected to the world around you. These apps include Weather, News, Finance, Travel, and Sports. They are essentially Internet feeds that are updated with new information when the tablet is connected to the Internet.

Each app has multiple screens that offer more detailed information. Swipe left or right to cycle through the app screens; you can also use semantic zoom to see a list of available screens—tap one to go directly to that screen. You can use the charms in these apps to search and share information.

In This Chapter

Weather

When you first launch the Weather app, you'll be prompted to allow the app to use your location. Tap the Allow button if you want it to use your location or the Block button if you don't. By allowing the app to use your location, weather updates for your area will appear on the live Weather app tile on the Start screen. You can also change your home location.

There are a total of five weather screens, which provide forecasts, a variety of weather maps, historical weather, and an advertisement. You can swipe left or right on the Surface tablet to cycle through the weather screens.

Weather home screen

The Weather home screen **A** displays the weather forecast. There are two actions you can perform immediately:

- **Extended forecast.** Tap the right arrow to see the forecast for the next five days. Tap the arrow again to return to the current forecast.

- **Additional weather reports.** Tap the down arrow to see additional forecast information. Tap the arrow again to hide that information.

Additional weather reports   *Extended forecast*

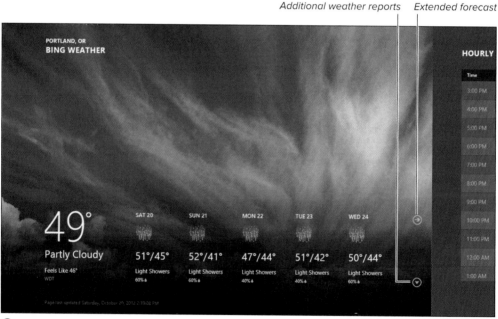

A Weather home screen

Hourly forecast

There's nothing to interact with on the hourly forecast screen. It is essentially a list of how the weather will change by the hour and includes time, temperature, and descriptive weather information such as rain, sun, light showers, the temperature it feels like outside, and the chance of precipitation.

Maps

There are 12 weather maps on the Maps screen. Tap a map to see a larger version of it. These maps are similar to those shown in news broadcasts on TV.

- **Regional Temperature.** Tap this map and tap the play button to see a short video showing regional weather changes over the next 24 hours.

- **Regional Doppler Radar.** Tap this map and tap the play button to see a short video showing weather patterns moving into the region over the next 24 hours.

- **Regional Precipitation.** Tap this map and tap the play button to see a short video showing regional precipitation over the next 24 hours.

- **Regional Satellite.** Tap this map to see a satellite snapshot of the weather, along with the date and time the screenshot was taken.

- **National Temperature.** Tap this map and tap the play button to see a short video showing national weather changes over the next 24 hours.

- **National Doppler Radar.** Tap this map and tap the play button to see a short video showing weather patterns moving into the country over the next 24 hours, with hourly changes.

- **National Precipitation.** Tap this map and tap the play button to see a short video showing expected precipitation across the nation over the next 24 hours.

- **National Cloud Cover.** Tap this map and tap the play button to see how the clouds will move across the nation over the next 24 hours.

- **National Satellite.** Tap this map and tap the play button to see a satellite view of how weather will move across the country over the next 24 hours.

- **Severe Weather Alerts.** Tap this button for a snapshot of the continental U.S. showing areas with severe weather alerts.

- **Airport Impact.** Tap this button for a snapshot of major airports across the country, with weather icons depicting how weather is affecting those areas.

- **Interstate Forecast.** Tap this button for a bird's-eye view of weather affecting the interstate highways.

Historical weather

This screen has an interactive graph and a snapshot of weather during the current month. The snapshot includes the average and record high/low rainfall, snow days, and rain days. The interactive graph shows weather broken down for a particular area by month over the past year. There are three buttons you can tap that change the graph:

- **Temperature.** Tap this button to see ranges in degrees so you can see which months were the hottest or coldest of the year.

- **Rainfall.** Tap this button to see how many inches of rain fell in a particular month.

- **Snow days.** Tap this button for how many snow days occurred in a particular month.

To use the Weather app bar:

The Weather app has a top app bar and a bottom app bar. They are the same across all the weather screens. Swipe up from the bottom or down from the top of the screen to access the Weather app bar **B** with the following options:

- **Home.** Tap this button to return to information about your home area.

- **Places.** Tap this button to see a list of location shortcuts. Tap the down arrow to display added places in the app bar.

  or

  Tap the location you want from the pre-qualified list of locations. The location is added to your Places list.

- **World Weather.** Tap to see a map of the world. Tap anywhere on the map to see a list of possible locations and current weather results for that area.

- **Change Home.** Tap this button to see a list of places listed as Favorites. Tap a place to save it as the Weather home screen.

  or

  Tap the *Add a new location* link to add another location. Type the name of the location (city or state) and then tap the Add button.

- **Current Location.** Tap this button to view the home screen with weather information for your current location.

- **Change to Celsius/Fahrenheit.** Tap to see temperatures in Celsius or Fahrenheit.

- **Refresh.** Tap to update the weather results.

B Weather app bar

To add weather places:

When you add a new location in Places, you can set it as Home, pin it to the Start screen, or remove it entirely. To add a new place, tap Places in the app bar and then tap the plus (+) tile. Type a new location, and tap the Add button. The new location appears in Places.

To manage weather places:

1. Swipe up from the bottom or down from the top of the screen, and tap the Places button.

2. Tap and hold a location to select it. An app bar appears with the following options:

    ▸ **Set as Home.** Tap the Set as Home button to make the location currently being viewed the Home location.

    ▸ **Pin to Start.** Tap this button to create a weather tile about this location on the Start screen. You can change the name of the location by tapping the text box and typing a new name. Tap the Pin to Start button to confirm. A new tile dedicated to weather in that location appears on the Start screen.

- **Remove.** Tap this button to delete the location from Places.

- **Add.** Tap this button to add a new location to Favorites. Type the name of the location (city or state) and then tap the Add button.

- **Current Location.** Tap this button to view the home screen with weather information for your current location.

- **Change to Celsius/Fahrenheit.** Tap to see temperatures in Celsius or Fahrenheit.

- **Refresh.** Tap to update the weather results.

TIP If you opted to allow the app to use your location, Weather will use it as the Home location.

TIP To view weather information for a saved location in Places, tap Places in the app bar and then tap that location button.

TIP The first location in Places will be the Home location that appears when you tap the Home button in the app bar or launch the app.

News

The News app is a feed of news stories by category: Top Story, U.S., World, Technology, Business, Entertainment, Politics, Sports, and Advertisement. You can also create your own news feeds or see stories from a particular news source.

To view news:

1. Tap the News tile on the Start screen. Swipe from right to left to scroll through news categories.

2. Tap a story to display it.

3. Swipe up from the bottom of the screen to access the app bar and display five options:

   ▸ Bing Daily (the News home screen; a drop-down menu has button shortcuts to news sections in the app)

   ▸ My News (the news feeds you create; a drop-down menu has button shortcuts to the news sections you created)

   ▸ Sources (the websites used to compile the news)

   ▸ Video (videos of news)

   ▸ Featured Sources (buttons to six popular news sites: AP, ABC News, the *New York Times*, Reuters, Fox News, and the *Wall Street Journal*)

(A) Adding a news topic to My News

(B) Pinning a source feed to the Start screen

To add a news section:

Sections are news feeds for a particular topic. You can also create your own.

1. Swipe down from the top of the screen and tap My News.

2. Tap the Add a Section tile.

3. Type in a news topic. A pre-qualified list of topics appears; tap one.

   or

   Type your topic, and tap Add (A).

   Stories about the topic appear in My News.

To view stories from news sources:

News stories are pulled from web sources ranging from *Time* magazine to *TV Guide*. You can view those sources and see more stories from those websites in the News app.

1. Swipe down from the top of the screen and tap Sources in the app bar. Swipe left or right to see sources grouped by category.

2. To see more stories from a site, tap a news source.

3. To create a tile on the Start screen dedicated to news from a source, tap a source, swipe up from the bottom of the screen, and tap Pin to Start in the app bar.

4. Tap the Pin to Start button in the pop-up (B). The source is pinned to the Start screen. You can also tap in the text box and type a new name for the source.

> **TIP** When reading an article in the News app, swipe up from the bottom of the screen and press Previous or Next to go to the previous or next news story.

Finance

The Finance app is a one-stop shop for financial news. The app has ten categories: Today, Indices, News, Watchlist, Market Movers, Across the Market, Magazine Articles, Rates, Fund Picks, and Advertisement. You can also convert currencies and add stocks to watch.

To use the Finance app:

1. Tap the Finance tile on the Start screen.

2. Swipe from right to left to see more categories. In this view, some categories are interactive. You can tap any tile on a category page.

3. Swipe down from the top of the screen to access the app bar **Ⓐ**. The Finance app bar gives you the following options:

   ▸ **Today.** Tap this to see financial results for the current day.

   ▸ **Watchlist.** Tap this to see a watchlist of stocks. You can add stocks to watch, and pin stocks to the Start screen. Tap the drop-down menu for buttons to stocks you added.

▸ **Market.** Tap this to see information on how the stock market performed. Tap the drop-down menu for buttons to World Markets, Market Movers, Currencies, Commodities, Bonds, and Fund Picks.

▸ **News.** Tap this for a financial news feed. Tap the drop-down menu for buttons to Top Stories, Business, Market, Technology, and Money.

▸ **Videos.** Tap this to see videos of financial news. Tap a video to play it.

▸ **Rates.** Tap this to see information on interest rates. Tap the drop-down menu for buttons to Mortgage Rates, Home Equity Rates, Auto Loan Rates, Savings Rates, and Credit Card rates. Tap a button for more details and rate information.

▸ **Best of Web.** Tap this button to see personal-finance stories. When you tap a tile, you will leave the app and be taken to the website of the tile you tapped.

▸ **Featured.** These are buttons to news sources. The sources will likely change, but for now they are the *Wall Street Journal*, CNBC, Reuters, WSJ Live, Bloomberg, Fox Business, and Benzinga.

Ⓐ App bar in Finance

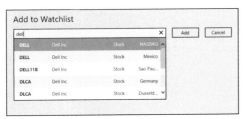

B Adding a stock to the watchlist

To add a stock to the watchlist:

1. Tap the Finance tile on the Start screen.

2. Swipe down from the top of the screen to reveal the app bar.

3. Tap the Watchlist button on the app bar.

4. Tap the plus (+) tile.

5. Tap the text box, enter the stock you want to add, and select the company from the pre-qualified list. Tap Add B.

TIP When adding a stock to the watchlist, you can enter either the company name or the stock exchange letters.

TIP To see exchange rates for currencies around the world in the Finance app, swipe up from the bottom of the screen and tap the Market down arrow on the app bar. Tap the Currencies button. Tap the Converter link in the lower-left corner of the Currencies screen. Use the drop-down menus to choose the currencies you want to convert, and enter an amount to see what it's worth in another currency.

Travel

The Travel app is designed to bring you information about vacation destinations. The app has seven categories: Today, Featured Destinations, Booking, Panoramas, News, Featured Videos, and Advertisement. You can learn more about destinations, view panoramic images, or book flight and hotels with this app.

To navigate the Travel app:

1. Tap the Travel tile on the Start screen. The Travel home screen features a spotlight destination.

2. Swipe from right to left to view more categories. Each screen provides different options:

   ▸ **Today.** This is a photo of a featured destination. Tap the "i" button to see where the photo was taken.

   ▸ **Featured Destinations.** There are tiles on this screen with photos and names of destinations. Tap a tile to learn more about it, including a descriptive overview of the location, currency, weather, flight finder, photos, panoramas, attractions, hotels, restaurants, and guides about things to do in that location. Tap any tile to read more.

   ▸ **Booking.** Tap one tile to search for flights, or tap the other to search for hotels.

   ▸ **Panoramas.** These are panoramas of specific locations at a destination. Tap a panorama tile and then swipe left, right, up, or down to see a 360-degree view. You can also pinch to zoom in or out to see more or less detail.

App bar in Travel

Viewing destinations by region

▸ **News.** Tap a tile to read an article about the destination.

▸ **Featured Videos.** Tap a tile to watch a video about the destination. When you tap to play a video, swipe down from the top of the screen to see the app bar. Tap Home to return to the Travel home screen.

To use the Travel app bar:

Swipe down from the top of the screen to reveal the app bar **A**.

- **Home.** Tap this button to return to the Travel overview.

- **Destinations.** Tap this button to see a wealth of destinations displayed on individual tiles **B**. Swipe from right to left to see destinations. Tap a tile to see more about the destination. Tap the back arrow to return to the Destination screen. To narrow down the list of places, tap the Show All down arrow and then tap a region (Africa, Asia, Caribbean, Central America, Europe, Middle East, North America, Oceania, and South America) **B**. Swipe from right to left to see more sub-categories: Top Trips, Up-and-Coming, and Hidden Gems.

- **Flights.** Tap the Flights button to search for and book flights. Tap the drop-down menu for Flight Search, Flight Schedule, and Flight Status buttons.

- **Hotels.** Tap the Hotels button to search for and book hotels in a destination.

- **Best of Web.** Tap this button and swipe from right to left to see a list of articles and websites. The categories are Frequent Travelers, Family Travel, Sustainable Travel, Tours and Cruises, Food and Wine, Road Trips, Budget Travel, Plan a Trip, Explore, and Travel Tools.

To book a flight:

1. In the Travel app, swipe down from the top of the screen to access the app bar.

2. Tap the Flight button. Tap Round-Trip or One-Way.

3. In the text boxes, enter where you're flying from and to, and when you want to depart and arrive.

4. To specify a cabin preference and number of travelers, tap the corresponding drop-down menus and tap an option.

5. Tap the *Search Flights* link **C**.

6. To sort the results, tap the down arrow next to Price, Airline, Return, Depart, or Stops.

7. Tap a flight to get more details, such as layover, flight duration, and the ability to book the flight **D**.

8. Tap the airline on which you want to book the trip.

9. Tap the Book button. You leave the Travel app and are taken to the airline website **E**.

C Search for flights

D Detailed information about flights

E Booking a flight

HOTELS

HOTELS

CITY

CHECK-IN
11/2/2012

ROOMS
1 room

October 2012

Su Mo Tu We Th Fr Sa

21 22 23 24 25 26 27
28 29 30 31
November
1 2 3
4 5 6 7 8 9 10
11 12 13 14 15 16 17
18 19 20 21 22 23 24
25 26 27 28 29 30
December
1

SEARCH HOTELS

F Finding a hotel

To search flight schedules and status:

1. In the Travel app, swipe down from the top of the screen to access the app bar.

2. Tap the Flight button.

3. To see flights by schedule, tap the Schedule tab, enter To and From information, and tap the *Get Flight Schedules* link. A list of available flights, stops, and days of week appears.

4. Tap the Status tab, tap the Airline box, and type an airline. A pre-qualified list appears in a drop-down box. Tap the airline you want, or keep typing.

5. Tap the Flight Number box, and type the flight number.

6. Tap the *Get Status* link to see flight information, such as flight status (landed, in transit, delayed) and arrival and departure details.

To book a hotel:

1. In the Travel app, swipe down from the top of the screen to access the app bar.

2. Tap the Hotel button.

3. Enter the city you want to book a hotel in. Tap the calendar in the Check-In and Check-Out text box, and tap the corresponding date in the calendar **F**. (You can also type in the date.)

4. Tap the boxes under Rooms and Guests for a pop-up box. Tap the number of rooms and guests, respectively.

5. Tap the *Search Hotels* link.

   A list of available hotels appears, along with price, hotel class, and amenities.

continues on next page

6. To filter the list by category, tap the down arrow next to Price, Hotel Class, or Amenities .

7. Tap the hotel that you want to book or see more information about.

8. Tap the Book button, and then tap the service you want to use to book the trip **H**. You leave the Travel app and are taken to that website.

To pin a destination to the Start screen:

1. Tap a destination in the Travel app.

2. Swipe up from the bottom of the screen to access the app bar.

3. Tap the Pin to Start button, and tap the Pin to Start button in the pop-up screen **I** to confirm. The destination appears as a tile on the Start screen.

> **TIP** When you tap a tile on the Best of the Web button in the app bar, you will be sent to a website. To return to the Travel app, swipe in from the left edge, drag the Travel app to the center of the screen, and release.

> **TIP** Rename a destination that you're pinning to the Start screen by tapping in the text box. Tap the X in the corner of the text box to delete the existing name, and type a new name.

> **TIP** Flight and hotel searches are powered by Kayak, so you can use only the websites that Kayak supports to book hotels and trips.

G Hotel options

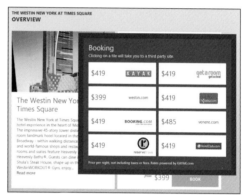

H Booking a hotel

I Pinning a destination to the Start screen

Sports

If you love Sports, this is the app for you. The app has eight categories: Top Story, Top Stories, Headlines, Videos, Slideshows, Schedule, Favorite Teams, and Advertisement. The meat of the app is found in the Sports app bar. It has shortcuts to every major sports league and provides in-depth information regarding that sport, such as news, schedules, standings, leading players, and leading teams.

To navigate the Sports app:

Tap the Sports tile on the Start screen. The Sports home screen displays a spotlight sports image. Swipe from right to left to view more categories.

- **Top Story.** This is an image of a high-lighted sports news story. Tap the "i" button to view the source of the photo. Tap the article's title to read the article.

- **Top Stories.** These are tiles of top stories. Tap a story's tile to see the full story. Tap the back arrow to return to the Sports home screen.

- **Headlines.** A list of sports-related head-lines powered by the Associated Press. Flick up and down on the headlines to view more. Tap a headline to see the full story.

- **Videos.** Tap a tile to watch the video. Tap anywhere on the screen to see the back arrow, video title, video playhead, and pause button. Tap the back arrow to return to the Sports home screen.

- **Slideshows.** Tap a tile to see the slide-show. Swipe from right to left to cycle through the pictures in the slideshow. Tap the back arrow to return to the Sports home screen.

continues on next page

- **Schedule.** This displays tiles of today's games by category. Information on the tile includes the teams playing, game time, and broadcast network. Tap a tile to view the website of the network broadcasting that game.

- **Favorite Teams.** Keep tabs on your favorite teams by adding them to the Favorite Teams list.

To use the Sports app bar:

1. Swipe down from the top of the screen in the Sports app to access the app bar. Swipe from right to left in the app bar to see more sports categories.

2. Tap a sports category shortcut **Ⓐ**. The default shortcuts are Today, Favorite Teams, NFL, NBA, MLB, NHL, Golf, Formula 1, Premier League soccer, La Liga soccer, All Sports, and Best of the Web.

3. Tap a league button. Detailed information about that league appears. Tap the drop-down menu to see buttons for Top Stories, Videos, Preview Articles, Recap Articles, Standings, Player Stats, and Team Stats.

4. Swipe from right to left to see information such as news, standings, players, leading teams, leading players, and schedule (if the sport is in season). Tap a tile on any of those screens to see more details.

5. Swipe down from the top of the screen to access the app bar. Tap the Best of Web button.

6. Swipe from right to left to see a list of articles and websites geared toward news and rumors, fantasy analysis, draft news, statistics, recruiting, sports business, podcasts, memorabilia, picks, and tickets and deals. Tap any tile to be taken to the corresponding website.

Ⓐ Sports app bar shortcuts

Add to Favorite Teams

Raide [×] [Add] [Cancel]

Oakland Raiders

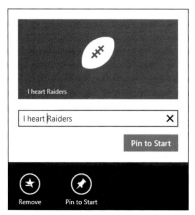

B Add a favorite team

I heart Raiders

I heart Raiders [×]

Pin to Start

Remove   Pin to Start

C Pinning a team to the Start screen

To add a favorite team:

1. Swipe from right to left until you see Favorite Teams on the screen.

   or

   Use semantic zoom, and tap the Favorite Teams tile in the Sports category tiles.

2. Tap the plus (+) tile. You can also swipe down from the top of the screen to see the app bar and then tap the Add button.

3. Type the name of your favorite team in the text box. A pre-qualified list of teams appears in a drop-down box. Tap the team you want in the drop-down box.

   or

   Type the full name of the team.

4. Tap the Add button **B**.

5. To see team information such as news, schedule, team leaders, team stats, and rosters, tap the newly created Favorite Team tile. Swipe from right to left and then tap a tile on any of those screens to see more details.

To pin a favorite team to the Start screen:

1. In the Sports app, swipe down from the top of the screen to access the app bar, and tap the Favorite Teams button.

   Team information appears.

2. Swipe up from the bottom of the screen to access the app bar.

3. Tap the Pin to Start button.

4. Change the name of the new tile by tapping the text box and tapping the X button to erase the team name. Type a new name, and tap the Pin to Start button in the pop-up screen **C**. The team appears as a tile on the Start screen.

continues on next page

To add or remove league shortcuts:

1. In the Sports app, swipe down from the top of the screen and tap All Sports.

2. Tap one or more tiles. A checkmark displays on the selected tiles. The app bar appears at the bottom of the screen **D**.

   ▸ **Clear selection.** Tap this button to deselect all selected leagues. A team is selected if it has a check mark in the upper-right corner of the tile.

   ▸ **Add.** Tap the Add button to add a selected league or leagues to the app bar.

   ▸ **Remove.** Tap a league, and tap the Remove button to remove the sports league from the app bar.

   ▸ **Leagues.** Tap a league to add it to or remove it from the app bar. When a league is in the app bar, you can tap the league's button to see detailed information about it.

TIP Tap the Refresh button in the bottom app bar to update the information.

TIP When you are viewing a sports page and don't know what a word means, swipe up from the bottom of the screen to access the app bar and then tap the Glossary button for a list of commonly used terms and their definitions.

Leagues

D Adding and removing leagues from the app bar

Windows Store and Games

The Windows Store is where you'll find apps for use with the Surface tablet. This includes things like productivity apps, sports apps, and book readers. (As of this writing, there is no bookstore in the Windows Store, so if you want to use the tablet as an e-reader and buy books, you'll need to download an app such as Kindle or Barnes & Noble's Nook from the Windows Store.) The Windows Store is also where you'll find updates for all the apps on the tablet—even those that came preloaded.

The Games app is similar to the Music and Video apps. Music and Video, however, have their own stores within those apps. The Games app has two stores: the Windows Games Store (it has connections to the Windows Store) and the Xbox 360 Games Store. The Games app is also where you can keep track of your Xbox 360 friends and your own player stats.

Windows Store

The Windows Store has a variety of apps available for free, for trial, or for purchase. Any apps that you download from the Windows Store can be installed on up to five Windows 8 devices. Downloaded apps are added to the last tile group on the Start screen. You can always move the tile to another position on the Start screen or add it to another tile group (See "Working with Tiles" in Chapter 2).

To navigate the Windows Store:

1. Tap the Store tile on the Start screen.

2. Swipe from right to left on the Store home screen to see more categories **A**. The categories are Spotlight, Games, Social, Entertainment, Photo, Music & Video, Books & Reference, News & Weather, Health & Fitness, Food & Dining, Lifestyle, Shopping, Travel, Finance, Productivity, Tools, Security, Business, Education, and Government.

A Windows Store home screen

3. Tap any tile with an app on it to see more about that app. Tap the Top Free tile to see the top free apps **B**, or tap the New Releases tile to see recently released apps **C**. Tap app tiles on those screens to learn more about an app or to install it.

continues on next page

B Top free apps

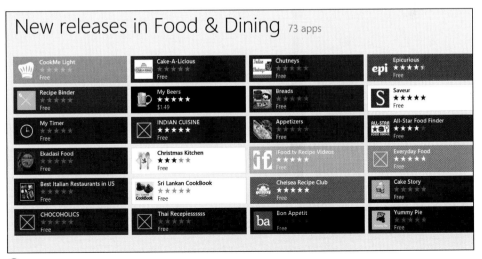

C New releases

When you tap an app tile, you'll see the app's details page 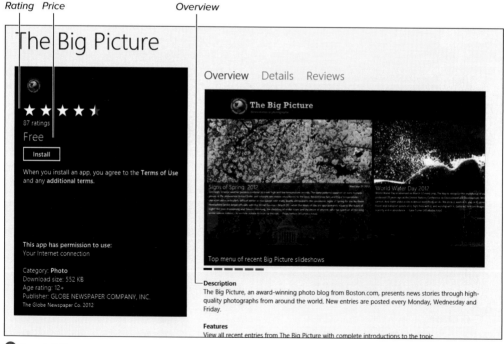.

- ▸ **Rating.** The app's overall rating, according to users.

- ▸ **Price.** Cost of the app.

- ▸ **Install.** Tap this button to download the app. If it's an app that you have to pay for, there will be buttons for Buy and Try (see "To purchase an app," later in this section).

- ▸ **Overview.** A screenshot of the app. Flick up to see the options Description, Features, Learn More (for a link to the app developer's website), and Report App to Microsoft (to report an app that violates the Windows Store's Terms of Use).

Rating *Price*   *Overview*

D App details page

E App reviews

▸ **Details.** Tap to see release notes, supported processors, supported languages, and app permissions.

▸ **Reviews.** Tap to see user reviews ⓔ. Tap the Sort By box to sort reviews by Oldest, Highest Rated, Lowest Rated, and Most Helpful. You can also rate a user review by tapping Yes or No next to "Was this review helpful?"

4. Swipe down from the top of the screen to access the app bar. There are two options: Home and Your Apps.

5. Tap the Your Apps button to see a list of all the apps installed on your tablet.

6. Tap the down arrow in the All Apps text box, and tap Apps Not Installed on This PC to see your apps that are not on the Surface tablet.

   or

   Tap Apps Installed on [*name of your tablet*] to see apps installed on the Surface tablet.

7. To sort app results by name, tap the Sort by Date text box and then tap Sort by Name.

8. Tap Home to return to the Store home screen.

To search for apps:

1. Swipe in from the right edge of the screen to reveal the Charms bar, and tap the Search charm.

2. In the Search box, type the name of the app you want to find; a pre-qualified list of results appears. You may also see a recommended app based on your search 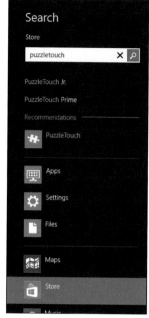.

3. Tap the search result you want; the app's details page appears.

4. If the exact result you want doesn't appear in the Search panel, then tap a similar search result. The screen will show possible app matches. Tap the down arrow in the text boxes for All Categories (a list of Store categories), All Prices (Free, Free and Trial, or Paid), and Sort by Relevance (Sort by newest, Sort by highest rating, Sort by lowest price, or Sort by highest price), and tap options in the text boxes to narrow the search results. Tap the tile of the app you want.

To install a free app:

1. Tap a free app's tile on the Store home screen.

2. Tap the Install button on the app's details page.

   The app downloads, and its tile appears on the Start screen.

F App search results

G Buy or try an app.

Payment and billing

○ American Express ✦

Add payment information

Credit card type *
● **VISA** ○ [MasterCard] ○ [AMERICAN EXPRESS] ○ [DISCOVER]

Credit card number *
[- Enter without dashes or spaces -]

Expiration date *
[MM ▼] [YYYY ▼]

Name on card *
[   ]

CVV *
[   ] What's this?

Billing address

H Payment and Billing screen

To purchase an app:

1. Tap an app's tile.

2. Tap the Buy button on the app's details page **G**. (You can also tap the Try button to download a free trial of the app to the Start screen.)

3. Tap Confirm to purchase the app.

   or

   Tap the Cancel button to cancel the purchase.

4. If you tapped the Confirm button, enter your Microsoft email account password and tap OK.

5. The Payment and Billing screen appears **H**. If you've already entered credit card or PayPal information, tap the circle next to the method of payment you want to use. Swipe up until you see the bottom of the screen, and tap Submit.

   or

   To enter new payment information, tap the circle next to the credit card type (Visa, MasterCard, American Express, Discover) you wish to use, and enter your information in the text boxes. Tap Submit.

   The app downloads and appears as a tile on the Start screen.

TIP When installing an app, click the Details tab on the app overview page and make sure ARM is one of the supported processors. That is the processor in the Windows RT tablet.

TIP Even if you start a search from a category page, it will search the entire Windows Store, not just the category.

Windows Store Charms

You can use charms to search and to change Windows Store settings. See "To search for apps," earlier in this chapter, to learn how to use the Search charm in the Windows Store. Use the Settings charm to make changes to your account, set search preferences, and get app updates.

To change account settings:

1. Swipe in from the right edge to access the Charms bar, tap Permissions, and tap Your Account Ⓐ. A screen with your account information appears Ⓑ.

2. To change your billing information, tap the *Edit payment method* link. You are taken to the Payment and Billing screen. Tap the circle next to the payment method you want to use, swipe up to get to the bottom of the screen, and tap the Submit button.

   or

   To enter new payment information, tap the circle next to PayPal or Credit Card and enter your information; tap Submit.

3. Tap the *View billing history* link to launch an IE browser window that displays a log-in window. Enter your Microsoft account and password to view your billing history.

4. To remove computers that can use the apps you downloaded, tap the Remove button under the name of the PC. Note that you can't add PCs here.

Ⓐ Settings panel

Ⓑ Your account settings

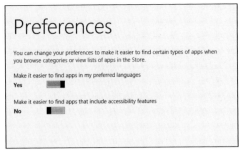

Preferences

You can change your preferences to make it easier to find certain types of apps when you browse categories or view lists of apps in the Store.

Make it easier to find apps in my preferred languages
Yes

Make it easier to find apps that include accessibility features
No

C Preferences

App updates

Automatically download updates for my apps
Yes

Check for updates

App licenses

If you're not seeing up-to-date info for the apps you own, try syncing app licenses.

Sync licenses

D App Updates settings

To change preferences:

1. Swipe in from the right edge to access the Charms bar, tap Permissions, and tap Preferences. The Preferences screen appears **C**.

2. Drag the "Make it easier to find apps in my preferred languages" slider to turn this feature on or off.

3. Drag the "Make it easier to find apps that include accessibility features" slider to turn this feature on or off.

To change App Updates settings:

1. Swipe in from the right edge of the screen to access the Charms bar, tap Permissions, and tap App Updates. The App Updates screen appears **D**.

2. Drag the "Automatically download updates for my apps" slider to turn this feature on or off.

3. Tap the Check for Updates button to immediately see if there are any updates available. If there are updates, tap the apps you want to update and then tap the Install button.

4. Tap the Sync Licenses button to see up-to-date information for the apps you own.

TIP To turn Windows Store notifications on or off, swipe in from the right edge to access the Charms bar and tap the Settings charm. Tap Permissions, and drag the slider to on or off.

Games

The Games app is tied to Xbox. It has its own Xbox 360 Games Store, and you can even view Xbox friends. To get the most out of the Games app, you'll want to be signed in to your Xbox account. There is also a Windows Games Store in the app. It contains additional games that aren't necessarily tied to the Xbox 360. Games in the Windows Games Store are also available in the Windows Store. If you download games from the Xbox 360 Games Store, you'll need to sign in to your Xbox Live account to see them in the Games app.

Even if you're not an Xbox gamer, you can use the Games app to keep track of and play games you download from the Windows Games Store. Typically, games downloaded from the Windows games Store can be played on the tablet but not on an Xbox 360.

To navigate the Games app:

1. Tap the Games tile on the Start screen.

2. Swipe from right to left on the Games home screen to see more categories . The categories are Player Details, Friends, Spotlight, Game Activity, Windows Games Store (this is the same as the Windows Store app), and Xbox 360 Games Store.

Ⓐ Games home screen

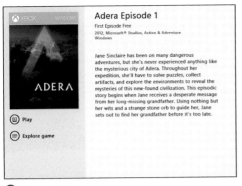

B Game details

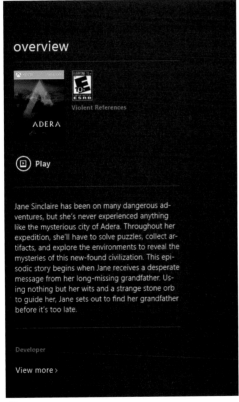

C Game overview

3. Tap any game tile to see its details screen **B**. Tap the Play button to play the game, or tap the Explore Game button to see the game overview screen **C**. The game overview screen provides an overview of the game, a rating, a Play button, and a *View more* link. Tap the *View more* link to see the game developer's details.

Some games will have more information available. Swipe from right to left to see additional information, such as Achievements and Leaderboards.

4. Tap the screen anywhere around the game detail pop-up to return to the Games home screen.

5. Tap any category to see more information about that category.

To sign in to the Games app:

1. There are two options for signing in to the Games app: Tap the *Sign in* link in the upper-right corner of the Games home screen, or tap the *Sign in* link on the "Check out what's happening on Xbox!" box on the far left of the Games home screen.

2. Enter the Microsoft email and password associated with your Xbox Live subscription; if you don't have an Xbox Live subscription, enter the Microsoft email and password associated with the Surface tablet. Tap Save.

3. If you have friends on Xbox, they appear in the Friends screen **D**. To invite friends, tap the Add Friend button. Type a friend's name or gamer tag in the text box, and tap Find. Their profile appears. Tap Add Friend.

To search for games:

1. Swipe in from the right edge of the screen to reveal the Charms bar, and tap the Search charm.

2. In the Search box, type the name of the game you want to find. Tiles of pre-qualified games matching your results appear on the screen **E**. Note that you will see results only from the Windows Games Store and Xbox 360 Games Store.

3. Tap the tile of the game you want. The game's details page appears.

D Xbox 360 friends

E Searching for games

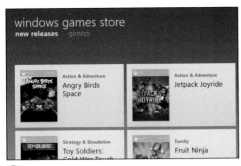

windows games store
new releases · genres

Action & Adventure
Angry Birds Space

Action & Adventure
Jetpack Joyride

Strategy & Simulation
Toy Soldiers: Cold War Touch

Family
Fruit Ninja

F Windows Games Store

To use the Windows Games Store:

Games in the Windows Games Store are also available in the Windows Store. You will be prompted to go to the Windows Store to download the game.

1. On the Games home screen, tap the "Find games at the Windows Games Store" button.

   or

   Tap the *Windows Games Store* link on the Games home screen.

2. Tap the *New Releases* or *Genres* link to see game tiles **F**.

3. Tap a game tile to see the game details.

4. Tap the Play button. A screen appears, prompting you to go to the Windows Store.

5. Tap the Store button to go to the game's overview page in the Windows Store. Follow the steps in "To install a free app" or "To purchase an app," earlier in this chapter.

6. The game downloads and appears as a tile on the Start screen. Tap the game tile to launch and play it.

   To connect the game to your Xbox Live account, enter your Xbox Live account email address and password on the Add Your Microsoft Account screen. The game appears under the Game Activity category.

To use the Xbox 360 Games Store:

The games in the Xbox 360 Games Store can be played only on the Xbox 360. You need an Xbox Live account to play any of these games.

1. On the Games home screen, tap the *Xbox 360 Games Store* link.

2. Tap New Releases, Top Selling, Top Rated, or Genres to see games in those categories .

3. To narrow your results, tap the *Games on Demand* link and then choose All Games, Arcade, or Indie from the drop-down menu.

G Xbox 360 Games Store

4. Tap a game tile to see the game details .

▸ **Explore game.** Tap this button to go to the game's overview screen. Swipe from right to left to see additional information, such as Extras, Achievements, and Related Games. These options will vary.

▸ **Play on Xbox 360.** To play on Xbox 360, you'll need the Xbox SmartGlass app, which is used to control your Xbox 360 from the Surface tablet. It also provides additional information about the game or app you're using. If you don't have SmartGlass, you will be prompted to get it from the Windows Store. Tap the Store button to be taken to the SmartGlass page in the Windows Store. This app allows you to use the Surface tablet as a second screen so you can interact with your Xbox 360.

▸ **Play trailer.** Tap this button to see a trailer of the game.

5. Tap the Play on Xbox 360 button.

6. To connect the game to your Xbox Live account, enter your Xbox Live account email address and password on the Add Your Microsoft Account screen. The game appears under the Game Activity category in the Games app.

TIP If this is your first time signing in to the Games app, take the time to customize your profile by tapping the buttons for Create Avatar, Edit Profile, and Share Profile. That way, you can easily interact with Xbox friends.

TIP Some games are available in both the Windows Games Store and the Windows Store. If you download a game that's available in both stores, when you first launch the game, sign in with your Xbox Live account to have the game appear under Game Activity in the Games app. Otherwise, you will need to go to the Start screen to play the game, and the game will not appear in the Game Activity category.

H Game details

Games Charms

You can use charms with the Games app to search, share your Xbox Live profile, and manage settings. See "To search for games," earlier in this chapter, to learn how to use the Search charm with the Games app.

To share your profile:

1. Swipe from left to right on the Games home screen until you see your player profile or friends. Tap the Share Profile button in either of those categories.

2. The Share panel appears **A**. Tap Mail or People. (Other apps you can share with may appear in this panel.) If you tap People, skip to step 4.

3. Tap the To box and type an email address. Tap the *Add a message* link, and type a message. Tap the Send button on the Mail panel **B** to send the email. Skip the following step.

4. Tap the down arrow and then tap either Twitter or Facebook. Tap the *Add a message* link, and type a message. Tap the Send button on the People panel to post **C**.

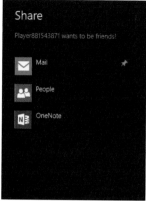

A Sharing an Xbox player profile

B Sending Xbox profile information

C Posting Xbox profile information

My Account

Sign Out

Xbox Membership
Xbox LIVE Silver Membership

Xbox Music Pass
30-Day Music Pass Trial

Manage Music Devices
More

Redeem Code
Redeem code for Xbox LIVE, Music Pass, or other items.

Manage Payment Options

Billing Contact Information

Billing History

Privacy and Online Settings

Contact Preferences

D Xbox account information

To manage your Xbox account:

The Account settings in the Games app are for your Xbox Live account, which is needed to play or purchase games from the Xbox 360 Games Store and the Windows Games Store. Some of the options will open an Internet browser window so that you can make changes online. (You'll notice that some of the settings refer to Music. The Music settings are strictly for music, not games.)

1. Access the Charms bar, tap Settings, and then tap Account. Options for managing your account display.

2. Tap the headings and green links in the My Account panel to access each account option **D**.

   ▸ **Sign In/Out.** Tap this to sign in to or out of your Microsoft account.

   ▸ **Xbox Membership.** Tap this to display your Xbox Live membership details. The content and options that are available to you depend on the type of membership you purchased.

   ▸ **Xbox Music Pass.** Tap this to see details about your Xbox Music Pass account.

   ▸ **Manage Music Devices.** Tap this to add or change devices that can access your Xbox Music Pass.

   ▸ **Redeem Code.** Tap this to enter a code or use Microsoft Points to redeem items from Xbox Live.

   ▸ **Manage Payment Options.** Tap this to change or add credit card billing information.

continues on next page

- ▸ **Billing Contact Information.** Tap this to change or add billing information.

- ▸ **Billing History.** Tap this to launch IE and display a log-in window for your Microsoft account and password so you can view billing history.

- ▸ **Privacy and Online Settings.** Tap this to sign in to Xbox, where you can change online and privacy settings.

- ▸ **Contact Preferences.** Tap this to receive or stop receiving Xbox newsletters.

3. Access the Charms bar, tap Settings, and then tap Preferences.

4. Drag the slider to turn on or off the sign-in prompt for purchases and account settings.

TIP **To turn Games notifications on or off, swipe in from the right edge to access the Charms bar and then tap the Settings charm. Tap Permissions, and drag the slider on or off.**

Camera

The Surface tablet comes with two cameras: a lower-resolution front-facing LifeCam camera and a higher-resolution camera on the back. The LifeCam is intended for taking self-portraits and for having video chats over Skype or other compatible applications. At the time of this writing, the video chat feature isn't available, but if you download an app such as Skype from the Windows Store, it should work with the LifeCam.

The rear-facing camera is for snapping pictures and shooting videos. In fact, the rear-facing camera is angled so you can use the kickstand to record events hands-free. Tap the Switch Camera button in the app bar and the tablet will automatically switch cameras. Pictures and videos taken using the Camera app are stored automatically in the My Pictures folder and are accessible via the Photos app.

In This Chapter

Taking Pictures

Opening the Camera app immediately launches the camera. The entire screen becomes the viewfinder. There aren't a lot of camera features, but you can set brightness, contrast, and resolution. The resolution options are based on what the camera on your tablet supports. All the camera controls are in Camera's app bar, which appears when the Camera app launches.

The Camera app has a built-in timer that allows you to delay taking a picture for three seconds, which is great for taking self-portraits.

To take a picture:

1. Tap the Camera tile on the Start screen.

2. Frame the shot, and tap anywhere on the screen except the grayed-out app bar **A**.

   The picture is saved to the Camera app and to the My Pictures folder in the Camera Roll folder.

To adjust camera settings:

1. On Camera's app bar, tap Camera Options.

2. Tap the down arrow under Photo Resolution to change the resolution **B**.

3. Tap the *More* link in the Camera Options pop-up to display more options **C**. Slide the Brightness bar left or right to adjust the brightness. Slide the Contrast bar left or right to adjust the contrast.

A Tap the screen to take a picture.

B Changing the photo resolution

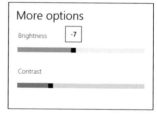

C Adjusting the contrast and brightness

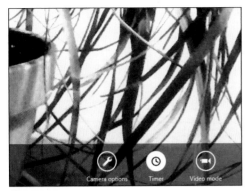

D Activating the timer

To set the camera timer:

1. In Camera's app bar, tap Timer **D**.

2. Tap the screen to start the three-second delay.

   The photo is captured when the timer countdown ends **E**.

3. To see captured photos, swipe from left to right or reverse-pinch.

E Timer countdown

Recording Video

The Camera app does double duty as a video recorder. As with the camera, there are limited features available.

Recording video is similar to taking a picture.

To record a video:

1. Tap the Camera tile on the Start screen.

2. Frame the shot, and tap Video Mode in Camera's app bar **Ⓐ**.

3. Tap the screen to start recording **Ⓑ**. Tap the screen again to stop recording. The video is saved to the Camera app and to the My Pictures folder in the Camera Roll folder.

To adjust video settings:

There are a few video recording settings available. All the controls are in Camera's app bar, which appears when the Camera app launches. Make sure Video Mode is highlighted in the app bar to change settings for the video recorder.

1. In Camera's app bar, tap Camera Options.

2. Tap the Video Resolution drop-down menu to change the recording resolution **Ⓒ**.

3. Tap the Audio Device drop-down menu to select how audio will be recorded.

4. Tap the More link to display more options. Slide the Brightness bar left or right to adjust the brightness. Slide the Contrast bar left or right to adjust the contrast **Ⓓ**.

Ⓐ Turning on the video recorder

Ⓑ Recording video

Ⓒ Changing the video resolution and audio device

Ⓓ Adjusting the contrast and brightness

E Turning on the timer

To set the timer:

The video recorder's built-in timer allows you to delay recording for three seconds.

1. In Camera's app bar, tap Timer **E**.

2. Tap the screen to begin the three-second delay.

   The video recording begins when the timer count is over.

3. Tap the screen to stop recording.

4. Swipe from left to right or reverse-pinch to see the recorded video.

TIP The Video Mode button allows you to switch between the camera and the video recorder. When the Video Mode button is highlighted, the video recorder is ready.

TIP When viewing pictures taken with the camera, swipe from right to left to reach the end of the camera roll so you can use the camera or video recorder again.

TIP View captured pictures or video by swiping left or right. To scroll through pictures quickly, zoom in and flick, and then tap the picture or video you want. Zoom out to see a carousel of your photos.

TIP If the Timer button is white, the timer is set; if the Timer button is transparent, the timer has not been set.

Working with Photos and Videos

There's not a lot that you can do with the videos and pictures that you take with the Camera app. However, you can crop or delete a photo and trim or delete a video.

You can determine whether a file is a video or a photo by looking for the timer and Play button in the lower-right corner of the screen: If you see the timer and the Play button, the file is a video; if you do not, the file is a photo.

To crop a photo:

1. With the Camera app running, swipe from left to right to view pictures and videos. Tap the photo you'd like to crop.

2. Swipe up from bottom edge of the screen to display Camera's app bar, and tap Crop. A crop frame with circles at each corner appears on the picture **A**.

3. Drag one of the circles on the crop frame to resize, and then release.

4. To crop something else in the picture, drag the crop box to another area of the screen **B**.

5. Tap OK to complete the crop and save the picture, or tap Cancel to remove the cropping parameters.

   Both the cropped image and the original image are saved in the Camera app and in the camera roll folder in the Photos app.

A Cropping a picture

B Moving the crop area

C Displaying a video

D Using the trim controls to define the new length of a video

To trim a video:

1. With the Camera app running, swipe from left to right to view pictures and videos, and tap the video you'd like to trim. The video displays **C**.

2. Swipe up from bottom of the screen to display Camera's app bar, and tap Trim. Small white circles appear at the start and end of the video counter.

3. Drag the white circle at the start of the video counter to the point where you want the video to start, and release; drag the white circle at the end of the video counter to the point where you want the video to end, and release **D**.

4. Tap OK in the app bar, or tap Cancel to remove the trim parameters.

   Both the trimmed video and the original video are saved in the Camera app and in the camera roll folder in the Photos app.

5. Tap the Play button to view the trimmed video.

To delete a photo or video:

1. With the Camera app running, swipe from left to right to view photos and videos, and tap the photo or video you'd like to delete.

2. Swipe up from bottom of the screen to display the app bar, and tap Delete 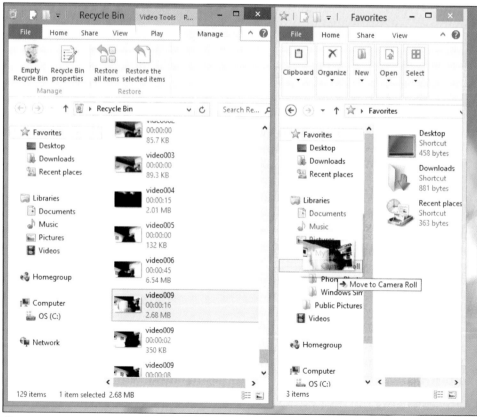.

   Deleting a photo or video moves it from the Camera app to the Recycle Bin. If you want the photo or video back, retrieve it from the Recycle Bin ⓔ.

TIP Drag the circle on the video counter left or right to change what footage is playing. This is called *scrubbing*.

ⓔ Retrieving a deleted video from the Recycle Bin on the Desktop

Share

Camera captured files

Email Joni Blecher
Mail

Email
Mail

Mail

SkyDrive

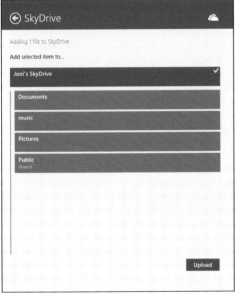

Ⓐ Sharing
a photo with
SkyDrive

Ⓑ Selecting a SkyDrive folder

Camera Charms

The only charms that work with the Camera app are Share and Settings. You can use them to share photos and videos and to turn the camera and microphone on and off.

To share a photo or video:

1. Swipe from left to right to see the camera roll, and tap the photo or video you'd like to share. Swipe in from the right edge of the screen to access the Charms bar.

2. Tap Share, and then tap SkyDrive or Mail **Ⓐ**. If you tap Mail, skip to step 5.

3. Tap the SkyDrive folder you want to upload the photo or video to **Ⓑ**.

4. Tap the Upload button on the SkyDrive bar **Ⓑ**. The photo or video uploads.

5. Tap the text box under the To heading, and type in the recipient's email address.

6. Tap Add a Subject, and type subject details for the email.

7. Tap Add a Message, and type a message.

8. Tap the Send button.

To turn the camera and microphone on or off:

1. Swipe in from the right edge of the Camera screen to access the Charms bar.

2. Tap Settings, and then tap Permissions.

3. Slide the Webcam and Microphone bar to the left to turn off the Camera app's access to the camera and microphone; slide it to the right to turn on Camera's access to those devices **C**.

TIP If you have devices connected to the tablet that can receive photos or videos, they appear under the Devices charm.

C Turning the Camera app's access to the camera and microphone on or off

12

Photos

The Photos app is a photo viewer and picture library. You can use it to view and do minor editing on photos stored on the tablet. You can also use it to view and share photos stored on SkyDrive, Facebook, Flickr, and devices.

In This Chapter

Pictures Library

The photos stored on the tablet are in the Pictures Library. When you take pictures using the Camera app, a Camera Roll folder is created in the Pictures Library. Photos attached to emails and downloaded from the Mail app are saved in the Pictures Library by default.

You can import photos from other devices, such as digital cameras, USB drives, microSD cards, and smartphones. When you use the Photos app to import photos, they too are saved in the Pictures Library by default.

To access the Pictures Library:

1. Tap the Photos tile on the Start screen.

2. Tap the Pictures Library tile on the Photos home screen. You'll see the Camera Roll folder. Pictures stored in the My Pictures folder also appear in the Pictures Library.

3. Swipe up from the bottom of the screen to access the app bar **Ⓐ**.

   ▸ **Browse by date.** Tap this button to view photos in the library by the month and year taken. To return to the folder view when browsing pictures by date, swipe up from the bottom of the screen to access the app bar and then tap the Browse by Folder button.

   ▸ **Slide show.** Tap this button to view photos as a slideshow. Swipe left or right to manually cycle through the photos.

   ▸ **Select all.** Tap this button to select all the photos in a folder.

   ▸ **Import.** Tap this button to import photos from another device, such as a digital camera, a phone, a USB drive, or a microSD card.

Ⓐ Pictures Library app bar

B Semantic zoom of photos

Choose a device to import from

If you don't see your device listed, make sure your device is turned on and connected to your PC.

| | MOT (G:) |

| | CD Drive (F:) MotoCast |

| | Removable Disk (H:) |

11

Browse by date   Slide show   Select all   Import

C Choosing a device to import photos from

Removable Disk (H:)

D Selecting and importing photos

4. Tap a photo to view it, or zoom in to see more photos on a single screen **B**.

5. When viewing a photo, swipe from left to right to return to the previous screen; swipe from right to left to go to the next screen.

To import photos into the Pictures Library from a device:

1. Attach the device to the tablet.

2. Swipe up from the bottom of the screen to access the app bar. Tap Import.

3. Tap the device on the pop-up menu **C**.

4. Tap Import Photos and Videos. Tap the photos you want to import. A check-mark appears in the upper-right corner of selected photos **D**.

5. Tap the text box at the bottom of the screen. Tap the X, and type a new name for the folder the photos will be stored in. Tap the Import button **D**.

   When the images are finished import-ing, you will see the message "Done!"

6. Tap the Open Folder button to see the imported photos.

TIP If you haven't yet used the Camera app, there will not be a Camera Roll folder. It's best to take a picture with the Camera app and let the system automatically create the Camera Roll folder.

TIP To play a slideshow of photos in a folder in the Pictures Library, tap the folder, swipe up to access the app bar, and tap the Slide Show button.

TIP If you have a lot of photos on a camera or USB drive and don't want to import them all, tap the *Clear selection* link and tap only the photos you want to import.

Working with Photos

There aren't a lot of editing options in the Photos app, but you can rotate and crop photos in the Pictures Library. These actions are not available for photos in the Facebook, Flickr, or SkyDrive folders. If you want to do more than rotate and crop, you'll need to download a photo-editing app from the Windows Store.

A Photos app bar

To use the Photos app bar:

1. Tap a photo in the Pictures Library.

2. Swipe up from the bottom edge of the screen to access the app bar A.

   ▸ **Set as.** You can set a photo as the lock screen image (tap the *Lock Screen* link), as the photo that appears on the Photos app tile (tap the *App Tile* link), or as the background of the Photos app (tap the *App Background* link).

   ▸ **Delete.** Tap to delete a photo. A pop-up window prompts you to confirm that you want to delete the photo. Tap the Delete button to complete the action.

   ▸ **Rotate.** Tap this button to rotate a photo clockwise in 15-degree increments.

   ▸ **Crop.** Tap this button to crop a photo.

B Cropping a photo

To crop a photo:

1. Tap a photo in the Pictures Library.

2. Swipe up from the bottom of the screen to access the app bar, and tap the Crop button. A box with four white circles in the corners appears.

3. Drag a circle to change the size of the crop box **B**. You can also drag the crop box to another area of the image.

4. To change the size of the crop box, tap the Aspect Ratio button and then tap Custom, Original, Square, Widescreen, 4x3, 4x6, 5x7, or 8x10.

5. To see the changes, tap the Apply button. Tap the Save Copy button to automatically save a version of the photo.

   or

   To start over, tap the Cancel button.

TIP Set the aspect ratio to Custom if you want to crop without constraints.

TIP A saved cropped photo appears in the same folder as the original photo.

Photos from Other Accounts

You can view photos from Flickr, Facebook, and SkyDrive by signing in to those accounts from the Photos home screen.

To view photos from other accounts:

1. Tap the Photos tile on the Start screen.

2. Tap the SkyDrive or Facebook tile Ⓐ. To view Flickr photos, skip to step 4.

3. Type your Microsoft email address and password in the text boxes, and tap Save. Tap Done on the next screen. Photos from your Facebook or SkyDrive account appear in a folder. (Note that if you haven't already signed in to Facebook in other apps on the tablet, you'll be prompted to enter your Facebook email address and password to allow the tablet to access photos.) Skip to step 9.

Ⓐ Tiles on the Photos home screen

Pictures library

B Play button

C Photo collage

4. Tap the Flickr tile on the Photos home screen.

5. Tap Connect.

6. Enter your Yahoo ID and password in the text boxes. Tap the Sign In button.

7. Tap the OK, I'll Authorize It button.

8. Tap Done.

9. To see a collage of all photos on the screen, tap the Play button **B** next to the Pictures Library tile on the Photos home screen **C**.

10. Swipe from left to right to return to the Photos home screen.

TIP To set a photo from SkyDrive, Flickr, or Facebook as the lock screen image, the image on the app tile, or the background photo in the Photos home screen, tap a photo, access the app bar, tap the Set As button, and make a selection.

TIP You can prevent a tile that connects to other accounts from appearing on the Start screen by tapping the *Hide* link in the upper-right corner of the tile. If you've already added photos to that tile, however, you'll need to make that change in Options settings. (See "To use the Settings charm," later in this chapter.)

Using Charms with the Photos App

You can use charms with the Photos app to find and share photos. You can also use the Settings charm to connect to or disconnect from other accounts.

To search for photos:

You can use the Search charm to search only for photos in your Pictures Library. You will need to be viewing the Pictures Library folder or the Photos home screen to search.

1. From the Photos home screen or the Pictures Library folder, swipe in from the right edge to access the Charms bar, tap Search, and enter a query .

   Possible search matches appear.

2. If you see one that fits, tap it.

Ⓐ Search Charm

To share a photo or video:

You can share any photo or video in the Photos app. This includes photos in the Facebook, Flickr, and SkyDrive folders. As you add to the tablet more Windows Store apps that work with the Photos app, those apps will appear in the Share panel.

1. Tap a folder tile in the Photos app, and swipe from right to left to find a photo or video. Tap the photo or video you'd like to share.

2. Swipe in from the right edge of the screen to access the Charms bar. Tap Share, and then tap SkyDrive or Mail Ⓑ. If you tap Mail, skip to step 5.

3. Tap the SkyDrive folder you want to upload the photo to.

4. Tap the Upload button. The photo uploads. Skip the following steps.

5. Tap the text box under the To heading, and type the recipient's email address.

6. Tap Add a Subject, and type a subject for the email.

7. Tap Add a Message, and type a message.

8. Tap Send.

To use the Settings charm:

The only settings you can change with this charm are account settings.

While on the Photos home screen, swipe in from the right edge to access the Charms bar, tap Settings, and tap the *Options* link .

- **Remove account.** Tap this button to prevent photos and videos associated with your Microsoft account from appearing in the Photos app.

- **Shuffle photos on the app tile.** Drag the slider right or left to turn shuffling photos on the Photos home screen on or off, respectively.

- **Show photos and videos from.** Tap the check box next to Pictures Library, SkyDrive, Facebook, Flickr, or Devices to show the corresponding tile on the Photos home screen. Tap the box again to remove the checkmark and remove the tile from the Photos home screen.

  Tap the *Options* link next to Facebook or Flickr to change what the tablet can access from those accounts.

TIP Information (metadata) in a photo file isn't used by the Search charm, so you'll need to know the filename of the photo you want to find in the Pictures Library.

C Account options

13

Video

The Video app is part of the Xbox Live experience; when you launch entertainment apps, you'll see the Xbox branding. The Video app is where you buy or rent movies and TV shows, but it is also where you play videos that you didn't get from the Xbox Video Store. And if you download apps such as Netflix from the Windows Store, they come with their own player.

If you connect an Xbox 360 or another supported device, you can stream movies and TV shows from the Surface tablet to that device. The Video app has a slick interface that works with the divider bar, so you can play videos in a smaller window while doing something else.

In This Chapter

Movies Store and Television Store

The Video app functions as both the video player for videos stored on the Surface tablet and as a place to buy or rent videos. The two functions share similar features when it comes to playing videos, but Xbox Video provides detailed information about the movies and TV shows in the store.

When you first open the Video app, you'll see a Spotlight section with tiles of featured movies and TV shows. Swipe from right to left to see the Movies Store and the Television Store. Swipe from left to right to see the My Videos folder. Tap to select.

When you launch the Video app, Xbox Video Store spotlights movies and TV shows available for rent or purchase, but you can also choose to view only your own videos (see "Using Charms with the Video App," at the end of the chapter). Later in the chapter, you'll learn how to import videos.

To explore movies:

1. Tap the Video tile on the Start screen. The Video home screen displays Ⓐ.

Ⓐ Video home screen

The Raven
2012, R, SD/HD, Thriller/Mystery, 1 hr 50 min

A brutal killing spree terrorizes 19th-century Baltimore and a young detective turns to a notorious author for help getting inside the mind of a serial killer in the stylish, gothic thriller, The Raven, an audacious reimagining of the lurid tales of Edgar Allan Poe. Starring John Cusack as the infamous inventor of the detective fiction genre and Luke Evans as an ambitious sleuth determined to stop more of Poe's gruesome stories from coming to chilling life—and death—The Raven weaves history and fiction into an original and twisted mystery worthy of the master of the macabre himself. When a mother and daughter are found viciously murdered in 19th-century Baltimore, Detective Emmett Fields (Evans) makes a startling discovery: the crime resembles a fictional murder described in gory detail in the local newspaper—part of a collection of stories penned by struggling writer and social outcast Edgar Allan Poe (Cusack). But even as Poe is questioned by police, another grisly killing occurs, also inspired by a popular Poe story. A deadly

- ⊛ Buy
- ⊛ Rent
- ☰ Explore movie
- ▶ Play trailer

B Movie details

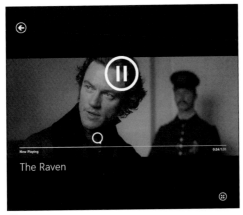

C Pausing a movie trailer

2. Tap a movie from the Spotlight section to display details about the video **B**. You have the options Buy, Rent, Explore Movie (takes you to the dedicated Movie page with an overview of the movie and a list of related movies), and Play Trailer. Tap the screen outside the video details box to close it and return to the grid of tiles.

   You can also flick from right to left to select from movies in the Movies Store.

3. Tap the Play Trailer button to watch the movie trailer. The Overview pane on the right has more movie options: Buy, Rent, and View More (to see a longer overview). You can also tap the Play Trailer button on the Explore Movie screen.

4. To pause the trailer, tap it and then tap the Pause button that appears **C**.

5. Flick from right to left to see related movies **D**. You can do this even while the trailer is playing.

6. Tap the left arrow to return to the Video home screen.

D Related movies

To explore TV shows:

You can buy complete seasons of TV shows or buy a season pass for TV shows currently airing. The season pass is available in SD or HD options.

1. Tap a TV show in the Spotlight section, or flick from right to left to view the Television Store, and then tap a TV show. The show details displays **E**.

2. Tap View Seasons **E**. An overview of the show appears in the right pane **F**.

3. Swipe from right to left to view the available seasons **G**.

4. Tap a season to display its details **H**. The detail screen gives you the option to buy the season or a season pass.

5. Swipe from left to right to return to the Video home screen.

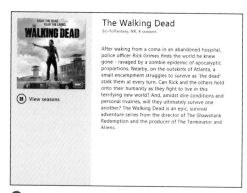

E TV show details

F TV show details page

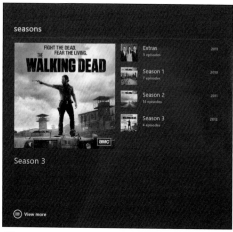

G Available TV seasons

H TV season details

❶ Movies Store

Rock of Ages
2012, NR, SD, Comedy, Romance, 2 hr 3 min

In 1987 Los Angeles at the height of glam rock, infamous and outrageous rock star Stacee Jaxx performs at Hollywood's legendary Bourbon Room club as it faces its final countdown. Meanwhile, an aspiring musician and a small town girl meet pursuing their dreams of music fame. The story unfolds through high energy dancing and heart-pounding hits of Def Leppard, Joan Jett, Journey, Foreigner, Night Ranger, REO Speedwagon, Pat Benatar, Twisted Sister, Poison, Whitesnake and more.

⊛ Buy

⊛ Rent

☰ Explore movie

▶ Play trailer

❶ Movie details

To buy or rent movies and TV shows from the Xbox Video Store:

You can buy or rent a movie or TV show, you can buy a complete season of a TV show, or you can buy a season pass for a current TV show so you can watch episodes currently airing. Whether you want to buy or rent a movie or buy a TV season or season pass, the steps to complete the purchase are the same. If you have an Xbox 360 connected, you can play any video on your tablet via your Xbox 360 and use the tablet to control video playback. You can also use the tablet to purchase a movie or TV and then access it directly from your Xbox 360.

1. On the Video home screen, flick from right to left and tap the *movies store* link.

2. Tap the *featured*, *new releases*, *top selling*, *genres*, or *studios* link to view movies in those categories. You can also flick right or left to quickly scroll through available movies listed under a specific category **❶**.

3. Tap a movie you want to buy or rent. The movie details display **❶**.

continues on next page

4. Tap the Buy button or the Rent button, tap either the SD Stream or the SD Download option, and then tap Next **K**.

   Viewing options (SD, HD, and so on) will change based on their availability for the movie you select.

   If this is your first time buying or renting movies from the Xbox Video Store, or you don't already have a credit card associated with your Microsoft account, the Add Your Microsoft Account screen displays; follow steps 5–8. Otherwise, skip to step 9.

5. Enter your Microsoft user name and password.

6. Tap the checkbox at the end of the Xbox Live Terms, and tap the I Accept button.

7. Tap the Add Payment Options button.

8. Enter your credit card type, credit card number, expiration date and year, card name, CW security code, and address; tap Save. Your default payment option is presented, along with options to "change payment option" or "use Microsoft points."

9. To change your credit card account information, tap the *Change Payment Options* link on the Confirm Purchase screen and follow the instructions in step 8 **L**.

10. Tap the Confirm button to complete your purchase. The movie downloads to the My Videos folder **L**.

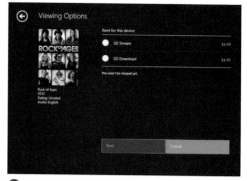

K Movie viewing options

L Confirming a movie purchase

To display the Video app bar:

If you have opened a video, you can always return to it while in the Xbox Video Store by swiping up from the bottom of the screen to display the app bar .

TIP To move forward or backward in a trailer, drag the video slider.

TIP You can change credit card information at any time by tapping Change Payment Options on the Confirm Purchase screen.

TIP Movie rentals are available for 14 days, but once you start watching the movie, the rental expires in 24 hours.

Buy/rent movies and TV shows to view on the Xbox 360

Currently playing movie

Rewind

Fast forward

The Raven
0:23/1:01

Get for Xbox 360 · Repeat · Previous · Play · Next · Play on Xbox 360

Play the movie again when it finishes

Play/Pause

Play movie on Xbox 360

 Video app bar

Open and Play Videos

The My Videos folder is linked to the Video app. If you store videos in that folder, you will see them listed under My Videos in the Video app. One of the easiest ways to add videos to the Video app is via SkyDrive. Since you can access SkyDrive on any device attached to the Internet, you can add videos from anywhere. (See Chapter 1 for more information about SkyDrive.) If you download videos from another site and they're not automatically added to the My Videos folder, you can move them manually using Windows Explorer on the Desktop; just drag the video from its current location to the My Videos folder. You can also use the Video app to open a video that's not stored in the My Videos folder. You can also open and play videos taken by the tablet's camera.

To play a video not stored in My Videos:

1. Open the Video app, and tap the *my videos* link.

2. If you don't have videos in the My Videos folder, tap the Open or Play Something button in the box under My Videos . Tap the Tell Me More button to find out how to manually add videos to the My Videos folder.

    or

    Swipe up from the bottom of the screen to display the Video app bar, and tap Open File .

A Prompts to open or play a video when the My Videos folder is empty

B Open File option in the Video app bar

G Folders and apps on the Surface tablet

D Camera Roll is where videos taken using the Camera app are stored.

3. Tap the down arrow next to Files. In the drop-down list that appears, tap the folder that contains the video you want to play **G**. Folders display **D**.

4. Tap Camera Roll **D**. The available videos display **E**.

5. Tap a video to select it, and tap Open. The video opens and plays **F**.

6. Tap the Home icon **F** to return to the Video home screen.

E Selecting a video to play

F Tapping the Home icon returns you to the Video home screen.

To add videos to My Videos from SkyDrive:

1. Tap the SkyDrive tile on the Start screen. Tap the folder on SkyDrive where your videos are stored. The contents of the folder display **G**.

2. Tap the video **H** you want to save to the My Videos folder. You can select more videos by tapping each file. To deselect a video, tap the checkmark in the corner of its tile.

   or

   Swipe up from the bottom of the screen, and tap Select All **H**.

G Videos on SkyDrive

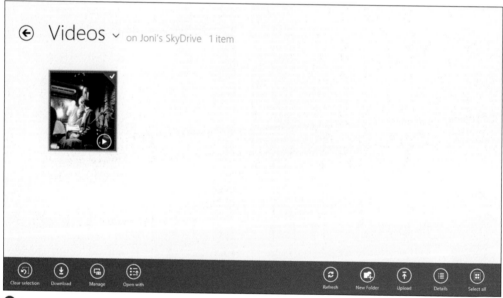

H Selected video on SkyDrive

3. Tap Download in the SkyDrive app bar.

4. Tap the down arrow next to Files, and tap Videos in the drop-down list to select the folder that you want to download the video file to .

5. Tap the Choose This Folder button, then tap OK. The video downloads to the My Videos folder.

6. Tap the Windows button on the tablet to return to the Xbox Video home screen. Flick from right to left to see the downloaded video under My Videos.

Ⓘ Download video to the Videos folder. This is the same as My Videos on the Desktop.

Ⓙ Downloaded video in the My Videos folder

Playing Videos

The Video app is also the video player. You can use it to open and play movies and TV shows purchased from the Xbox Video Store or to play videos stored in other places on your tablet. The Video app works with the divider bar, so you can play a video in a smaller window even while you're using another app on the tablet.

The app bar has all the controls you need to play videos.

To play a video:

1. Tap the Video tile on the Start screen. The Video app displays.

2. Flick from right to left, and tap the *my videos* link to see the videos in the My Videos folder .

3. Tap a video, and it starts playing.

4. Swipe up from the bottom of screen to access the Video app bar . The app bar contains all the video controls.

   ▸ **Previous.** Tap this button to go to a previous video chapter.

   ▸ **Pause/Play.** Tap to pause the video. When a video is paused, the icon changes to a Play icon. Press Play to resume playing the video.

   ▸ **Next.** Tap Next to go to the next video chapter.

   ▸ **Play To.** If you have the tablet attached to a device that can receive video, such as an Xbox 360, tap this button to send the video to that device.

   ▸ **Playback options.** Tap this button and then tap Repeat to play the video again; or tap Closed Captioning for that option.

Ⓐ My Videos folder

Ⓑ Video app bar

C Use the video slider to move between video frames.

5. Tap the screen while a video is playing to display the video slider. Drag the video slider to move forward and back in a playing video **C**.

To play a video while using another app:

If you're in an app and want to watch a video, you can use the divider bar to launch the Video app.

1. Tap the Video tile on the Start screen.

2. Tap the Windows button on the tablet, and tap another app.

3. Drag in from the left edge of the screen, and release when the divider bar appears and the Video application snaps into a third of the screen **D**. The most recent video you were watching will appear in the panel. Tap the Play button to play the video.

4. Drag the divider bar to the left to remove the video player pane.

TIP When viewing the Video app in the left or right pane, you can play the most recently accessed video. If you want to do more, such as pick another video or play a larger version of the video, drag the divider bar so that the Video app takes up at least two-thirds of the screen.

D Video playing while using SkyDrive

Using Charms with the Video App

The Search, Share, and Settings charms work with the Video app. Use the Settings charm to set account information and preferences. Use the Search charm to find movies and TV shows available to buy or purchase. Use the Share charm to share movie and TV show information from the Xbox Video Store with others.

To search for movies or TV shows:

1. Within the Video app, access the Charms bar and tap Search **Ⓐ**.

2. Type a query in the search text box **Ⓑ**. A list of movies and TV shows displays as you type. Or you can tap the magnifying glass icon to perform the search for the entered text.

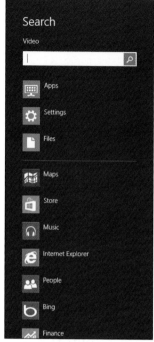

Ⓐ Video Search panel

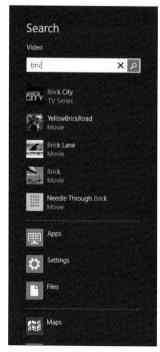

Ⓑ Searching for movies and TV shows in the Video app

3. Tap a search result listed under the search text box. The movie or TV show appears .

C Selected search result

To share video information with others:

You can use the Share charm to share information provided by the Xbox Video Store, but as of this writing, you can't send video files to others.

1. Tap a movie or TV show that you want to share information about. Access the Charms bar, and tap Share.

2. Tap a method by which to share information 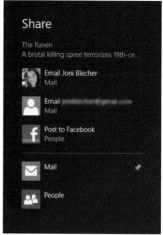. Your options include Facebook, Mail, and People. (If you want to share to other social media accounts connected in your People app, choose People.)

3. In the Add a Message text box, type the message you want to add to what you're sharing 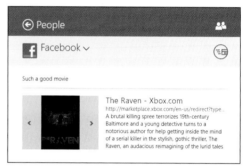.

4. Tap the down arrow next to Facebook, and choose Facebook, Twitter, or another connected social media site that can share this information. Tap the Send button to share the post .

D Share panel

E Share to social media accounts using People.

F Select a social media site and post to it.

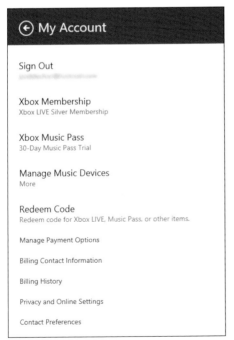

G Settings panel

H My Account settings

To access Xbox settings:

The Account settings in the Video app are for your Xbox Live account, which is needed to rent or purchase content from the Xbox Video Store. Most of the options take you to the Internet so that you can make changes online. (You'll also notice that some of the settings refer to Music. The Music settings are strictly for music, not video.)

1. Access the Charms bar, tap Settings, and then tap Account **G**.

2. Tap the headings and red links in the My Account bar to access each account option **H**.

   ▸ **Sign In/Out.** Tap this to sign in to or out of your Microsoft account.

   ▸ **Xbox Membership.** Tap this to display your Xbox Live membership details. The content and options that are available to you depend on the type of membership (Gold or Silver) you purchased.

   ▸ **Xbox Music Pass.** Tap this to listen to and download music on your devices.

   ▸ **Manage Music Devices.** Tap this to add or change devices that can access your Music Pass.

   ▸ **Redeem Code.** Tap this to enter a code to redeem items from Xbox Live.

   ▸ **Manage Payment Options.** Tap this to change or add credit card billing information.

   ▸ **Billing Contact Information.** Tap this to change or add billing information.

continues on next page

- **Billing History.** Tap this to launch Internet Explorer and display a log-in window for your Microsoft account and password so you can view billing history.

- **Privacy and Online Settings.** Tap this to sign in to Xbox, where you can change online and privacy settings.

- **Contact Preferences.** Tap this to receive or stop receiving Xbox newsletters.

To change Preferences settings:

Use these settings to manage how the Video app works for you.

Access the Charms bar, tap Settings, and tap Preferences ❶.

- **My Videos.** Tap the *Tell me more* link for help with how to add videos to the My Videos folder. (It will be similar to the process described in "To add music from other Desktop folders" in Chapter 14.)

- **Startup view.** Drag the slider to On to have the Video app open the My Videos folder when it launches.

- **Confirm purchases.** Drag the slider to On to receive a prompt before completing the purchase of a movie or TV show.

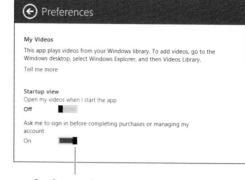

Confirm purchases

❶ Video preferences

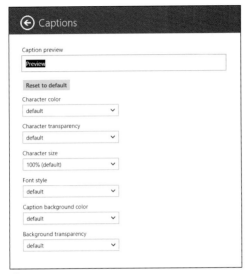

Caption preview

Preview

Reset to default

Character color
default

Character transparency
default

Character size
100% (default)

Font style
default

Caption background color
default

Background transparency
default

J Caption options

To change caption settings:

You can change the appearance of a movie's or TV show's captions. (Note that not all movies and TV shows make captions available.)

Access the Charms bar, tap Settings, and tap Captions **J**.

- **Caption preview.** The changes you make in the Captions settings appear in the Caption Preview text box.

- **Character color.** Tap the down arrow and tap a color (white, black, red, green, blue, yellow, magenta, or cyan) to change the text color.

- **Character transparency.** Tap the down arrow and tap Solid or Semitransparent to choose a level of transparency.

- **Character size.** Tap the down arrow and tap a percentage (50%, 100%, 150%, or 200%) to choose the text size.

- **Font style.** Tap the down arrow and tap a font (monospaced with serifs, proportionally spaced with serifs, monospaced without serifs, proportionally spaced without serifs, casual, cursive, or small capitals).

- **Background color.** Tap the down arrow and tap a color (white, black, red, green, blue, yellow, magenta, or cyan) to change the background color surrounding the text.

- **Background transparency.** Tap the down arrow and tap Solid or Semitransparent to choose the level of transparency surrounding the text.

To change notification settings:

1. Access the Charms bar, tap Settings, and then tap Permissions 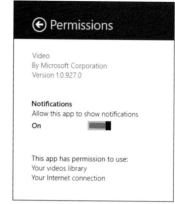.

2. Drag the slider on or off to receive or prevent notifications.

TIP Even though there are account settings for Xbox Music listed in the Accounts charm, signing up for Xbox Music will not get you a movie or TV show pass.

TIP Xbox Live lets you buy and rent movies and TV shows directly from your Xbox 360.

⊕ Permissions

Video
By Microsoft Corporation
Version 1.0.927.0

Notifications
Allow this app to show notifications
On

This app has permission to use:
Your videos library
Your Internet connection

Ⓚ Turn notifications on or off in the Permissions settings.

14

Music

When you launch entertainment apps, you'll see the Xbox branding. The Music app is where you buy music, but it is also where you play your music. It has a slick interface that works with the divider bar, so you can snap the app and control music while using another app on the tablet.

Although the interface is sharp—with album art and music tiles—there are some maneuvers that feel reminiscent of the previous Windows media players. For example, it's not immediately clear how to add music to your My Music folder. You will need to access the traditional file structure on the Desktop to make music accessible from the Music app.

In This Chapter

Music Store

The Music app functions as both the music player for the Surface tablet and as the storefront for the Xbox Music Store (where you can buy music). The two functions share similar features when it comes to playing music, but the Xbox Music Store provides more detailed information about artists. If you want to learn more about an artist in your My Music folder, you can use the Search panel to search the Xbox Music Store.

The first thing you see when you open Music is the Xbox Music Store, but you can change that (see "Using Charms with the Music App," at the end of this chapter). Later in the chapter, you'll learn how to import your music so you can listen to it using the Music app.

As you fill up your My Music folder, the app shows what music you have and highlights what is currently playing. If you're looking for new music, swipe from right to left to see highlighted artists in the store. The Music home screen displays music grouped by artist in the Xbox Music Store and lists top albums and artists. It also provides one-touch access to Smart DJ and your playlists.

To explore Music:

1. Tap the Music tile on the Start screen. The Xbox Music screen displays **Ⓐ**.

2. Tap an artist. Songs by that artist display.

3. Tap a song **Ⓑ**.

4. Tap Play to play the song, tap Buy Song to purchase it, or tap Add to My Music to add it to your My Music folder **Ⓑ**. (Note that these options will vary.) Under the album art, you'll notice the options Play Album, Buy Album, and Explore Artist.

Ⓐ Music home screen

Ⓑ Album songs

bio

▶)) Play Smart DJ

Hailing from South London, Florence Mary Leon-
tine Welch writes songs that occupy the same
confessional territory as gossip-loving, genre-
bending contemporaries like Amy Winehouse,
Kate Nash, Adele, and Lily Allen and the moody,
classic art rock of Kate Bush, blending pop, soul,
and baroque arrangements into a sound that
earned the young artist considerable buzz in
2007. Managed by the Camden-based DJ duo the
Queens of Noize and backed by a rotating lineup
of musicians, Florence + the Machine released
their debut single, "Kiss with a Fist," on the Moshi
Moshi label in June 2008. The critically acclaimed
debut album Lungs followed in July 2009 and
quickly became one of the year's most popular
releases in the U.K., where Florence charted four
Top 40 singles in less than 12 months. The songs
gathered steam in other parts of the world, too,
particularly in America, where "Dog Days Are
Over" peaked at number 21, went platinum, and
even earned its own performance on the TV show
Glee. Lungs was reissued the following year in a
two-disc package entitled Between Two Lungs,
and included a bonus 12-track disc that featured

View more >

C Artist bio

D More albums by the selected artist

5. Tap Explore Artist **B**. Information about the artist displays. You can tap the *View more* link under the artist's bio for more information **C**.

6. Swipe from right to left to see other albums by the selected artist **D**.

continues on next page

7. Tap the *View all albums* link to see all albums by the artist. Tap the down arrow next to Release Year to sort by popularity **E**.

8. Tap the left arrow to return to the music, or tap the X in the upper-right corner to exit overview view.

9. Tap the *Show song list* link on the artist's main page to see all songs **F**.

10. Tap a song to play it **G**.

E Sort albums by release date or popularity

F More artist options

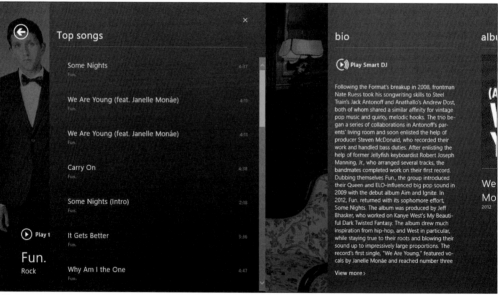

G More songs by artist

featured ∨

| featured |
| new releases |
| top |

Classical

Comedy / Spoken Word

Country

Electronic / Dance

Hip Hop

Jazz

Hello My Name
Bridgit Mendler

Don't Make Em
Ne-Yo

Epidemia
Ill Niño

House of Gold
Stone Sour

For All
Far East Movement

 Sort songs by the Featured, New Releases, or Top categories.

To use the Xbox Music Store:

The Music app is also a store where you can purchase songs or albums by any artist featured in the Music app.

1. Tap the *all music* link Ⓐ on the Xbox Music home screen.

2. Tap the down arrow next to Featured to sort by Featured, New Releases, or Top Ⓗ.

3. Tap a genre in the left pane to see sub-categories of that genre.

   You can also sort by Featured, New Releases, or Popular within subcategories.

To search the Xbox Music Store:

1. Swipe in from the right edge of the screen to display the Charms bar, and then tap Search.

2. Type a query in the Search box to find a specific artist ❶. A list of artists displays as you type.

3. Tap a song or album you want to purchase, and then tap Buy Album or Buy Song ❶.

   If this is your first time buying music from the Xbox Music Store, follow steps 4–8. If not, skip to step 9.

4. Enter your Microsoft user name and password.

5. Tap the checkbox for Xbox Live Terms of Use, and tap I Accept.

6. Tap the Add Payment Options button.

❶ Searching by artist

❶ Buying music

K Adding credit card information

7. Enter your credit card type, credit card number, expiration date and year, card name, CW security code, and address. Tap Save **K**.

8. Tap the Purchase button.

9. To change your credit card account information, tap the *Change Payment Options* link on the Confirm Purchase screen and follow the instructions in step 7.

10. Tap Confirm to complete your purchase **L**. The music downloads to the My Music folder.

TIP You can play a song by tapping the **Add to Now Playing** button in the lower-left of the **Music app bar.**

TIP You can change credit card information at any time by tapping **Edit or Add a New Credit Card** under **Change Payment Options** on the **Confirm Purchase screen.**

TIP If you have an **Xbox Music Pass**, there is only an option to download the music (there is no option to buy the music). Tap the **Download Music button** on the music preview screen to add the music to your **My Music folder.**

L Completing a purchase

Adding Music to the Music App

One of the easiest ways to add music to the Music app is via SkyDrive. Since you can access SkyDrive on any device attached to the Internet, you can add music from anywhere. (See Chapter 1 for more information about SkyDrive.) If you download music from another site and it's not automatically added to the My Music folder, you'll need to move it manually via the Desktop.

To add Music from SkyDrive:

1. Tap SkyDrive on the Start screen, and tap the SkyDrive folder where your music is stored. The contents of the folder display **Ⓐ**.

2. Swipe up from the bottom of the screen, and tap Select All in the app bar. All the files are selected **Ⓑ**.

   You can also tap a single file or multiple files.

Ⓐ Music folder on SkyDrive

Ⓑ Selecting all the files in the folder

Documents

Pictures

Music

Videos

Desktop

Downloads

Homegroup

Computer

Network

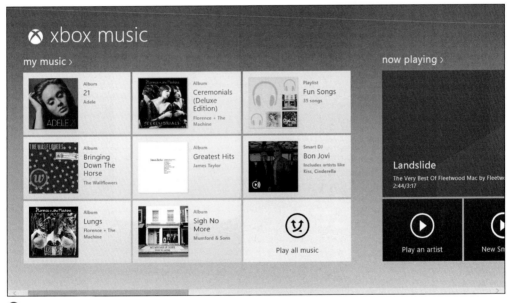

C Selecting
the Music folder

3. Tap Download in the Music app bar.

4. Tap the down arrow next to Files, and tap Music in the drop-down list **C**.

5. Tap the Choose This Folder button.

6. Tap OK. The music downloads to the Music folder.

7. To access the Music app, swipe in from the left edge of the Music screen and drag Music toward the center.

8. Swipe from left to right **D** and tap the *my music* link to see the downloaded music.

xbox music

my music >

now playing >

Album
21
Adele

Album
Ceremonials (Deluxe Edition)
Florence + The Machine

Playlist
Fun Songs
35 songs

Album
Bringing Down The Horse
The Wallflowers

Album
Greatest Hits
James Taylor

Smart DJ
Bon Jovi
Includes artists like Kiss, Cinderella

Landslide
The Very Best Of Fleetwood Mac by Fleetwo
2:44/3:17

Album
Lungs
Florence + The Machine

Album
Sigh No More
Mumford & Sons

Play all music

Play an artist

New Sn

D My Music

To add music from other Desktop folders:

When you download music from other devices, the music might be saved in a folder other than My Music (such as Downloads); you need to move it to your My Music folder if you want to access it from the Music app. To move the files, you need to use the Desktop interface.

1. Tap the Desktop tile.

2. Tap Windows Explorer .

3. Tap the Music folder in the left column of Windows Explorer to reveal subfolders.

4. Tap the Downloads folder in the left column of Windows Explorer, and locate the music file you want to move.

5. Drag the file to the My Music folder in the left column 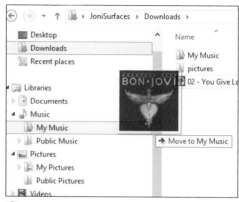.

6. Swipe in from the left edge of the tablet , and drag the Music app toward the center of the tablet to open it. The music file you moved appears in the My Music folder in the Music app.

TIP Take the time to select the My Music folder when you download music; otherwise, you will need to move downloaded music to the My Music folder manually.

E Launching Windows Explorer

F Moving a song to the My Music folder

G Accessing the Music app from the Desktop

(A) My Music folder

Playing Music

While in the Music app, you can scroll through the Music home screen to view your music, create playlists, and play your music.

To play music:

The app bar has all the controls you need to play music and create playlists.

1. Tap the Music tile on the Start screen. The Music app displays **(A)**.

2. Tap the *my music* link to see the music in the folder **(B)**.

3. Tap a song in your My Music folder, and tap the Play button. Tap the Add to Now Playing button to see the song in the Music tile on the Start screen **(B)**.

continues on next page

(B) Playing a song

4. Swipe up from the bottom of screen to access the app bar **C**. The app bar gives you several options for managing and playing your songs.

- ▶ **Add to [*playlist name*].** The name of your most recently accessed playlist appears on this button; tap it to add the currently playing song to that playlist.

- ▶ **Add to playlist.** Tap this to add the song to an existing playlist or to create a playlist.

- ▶ **Play Smart DJ.** The Smart DJ creates playlists based on a particular artist. Tap this button to create a Smart DJ playlist based on the current song.

- ▶ **Play on Xbox 360.** Tap to play on a connected Xbox 360.

- ▶ **Delete.** Tap to delete the selected song.

- ▶ **Properties.** Tap to view metadata about the song, such as artist, title, album title, genre, and length.

- ▶ **Song currently playing.** Tap this button to launch a larger player, which is helpful if you want a less cluttered view. It has buttons for Previous/Next song and Play/Pause. It also shows where you are in the song, the artist, and the song name. Swipe right to return to the previous screen. Tap the screen for buttons that allow you to show more info about the song or to show the song list.

- ▶ **Previous.** Tap this button to go to the previous song.

- ▶ **Pause/Play.** Tap to pause the song. When a song is paused, the icon changes to a Play icon. Press Play to resume playing the song.

- ▶ **Next.** Tap to go to the next song on the playlist.

- ▶ **Playback options.** Tap for a pop-up menu: tap Shuffle to shuffle songs, or tap Repeat to repeat the song.

Song currently playing

C Music app bar

D Changing the music list view

E Playing an album

5. Tap the down arrow below the "songs arranged by" label to display options for how songs appear in the My Music folder in the Music app. The options are Date Added, A to Z, Genre, Artist, and Album **D**.

6. Tap Album in the drop-down list, and tap an album title. A pop-up displays the songs on the album.

7. Tap Play Album to play the music on the selected album **E**.

To view the large music player:

If you don't want to see the list of songs while playing a song, you can launch the large music player.

1. Tap the Music tile on the Start screen.

2. Tap My Music to see music in your folder ⓑ.

3. Tap a song, and tap Play ⓑ.

4. Swipe up to display the app bar, and tap the song playing in the app bar. The large player appears on the screen.

    The majority of the large music player screen is occupied by basic music controls, including a music slider for moving forward or back in the song. The right panel provides additional information about the artist.

5. Tap the flower icon in lower-right corner to hide song details ⓕ.

ⓕ Hiding song details in the large music player

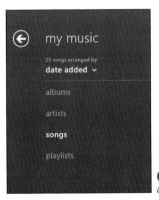

now playing

Livin' On A Prayer — 4:10
Bon Jovi

Livin' On A Prayer (Album Version) — 4:09
Bon Jovi

You Give Love A Bad Name (Album Version) — 3:42
Bon Jovi

It's My Life (Album Version) — 3:44
Bon Jovi

We Weren't Born To Follow (Album Version) — 4:03
Bon Jovi

I'll Be There For You (Album Version) — 5:46
Bon Jovi

Born To Be My Baby (Album Version) — 4:40
Bon Jovi

G Upcoming songs list

my music

25 songs arranged by
date added ˅

albums

artists

songs

playlists

H Creating
a playlist

my music

⊕ new playlist

Save

0 playlists arranged by
date changed ˅

albums

artists

songs

playlists

I Naming a playlist

---

6. Tap the *Show song list* link in the lower-left corner to see a list of the upcoming songs **G**.

To create a playlist:

1. Tap the *my music* link on the Music home screen.

2. Tap Playlists **H**.

3. Tap the New Playlist button. Type a name for the playlist in the text box **I**, and tap the Save button.

4. In the My Music menu, tap Songs.

5. Tap the song you'd like to add to the playlist.

6. Swipe up from the bottom of the screen, and tap the Add to Playlist button to choose a playlist or to create a new one.

TIP Shuffling songs will not reorder them on the screen.

TIP If you view songs by genre, artist, or album and then tap Shuffle, only songs in the selected category will shuffle.

TIP If you have connected the tablet to an Xbox, there will be an option that allows you to stream music over the Xbox.

Using Charms with the Music App

The Search, Share, and Settings charms work with the Music app. Use the Settings charm to set account information and preferences. Use the Search charm to find songs (also see "To Search the Xbox Music Store," earlier in this chapter). Use the Share charm to share music information with others.

To search for music:

1. Within the Music app, access the Charms bar and tap Search .

2. Type a query in the Search text box **B**.

3. Tap a Search result from the results listed under the Search query box. A bio of the artist appears **C**.

Ⓐ Search charm

Ⓑ Searching for music

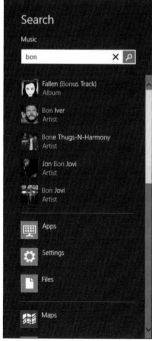

Ⓒ Selecting a search result

Share

Jon Bon Jovi
Jon Bon Jovi spent most of the 1980s e...

Email Joni Blecher
Mail

Email
Mail

Post to Facebook
People

Mail

People

D Share charm

E Sharing with Facebook

F Settings charm

To share music information with others:

You can share music information with others, but as of this writing, you can't send music files to others using the Share charm.

1. Access the Charms bar, and tap Share **D**.

2. Tap a method by which to share information **E**. Your options include Facebook, Mail, and People. (Select People if you want to post the information to social media accounts connected to your People app.) Note that if you have other apps that can share Music information, they will appear.

3. In the Add a Message box, type a message to add to your post.

4. Tap the Send button to send the post.

To access Xbox settings:

The Account settings in Music are for your Xbox account, which is needed to make the most of Music. Most of the options take you to the Internet so that you can make changes online.

1. Access the Charms bar, tap Settings, and then tap Account **F**. Options for managing your account display.

continues on next page

2. Tap the headings and red links in the My Account bar to access each account setting option .

- ▸ **Sign In/Out.** Tap this to sign in to or out of your Microsoft account.

- ▸ **Xbox Membership.** Tap this to display your Xbox Live membership details. The content and options that are available depend on the type of membership you purchased.

- ▸ **Xbox Music Pass.** If you had a Zune Music Pass, it will now be an Xbox Music Pass. With the pass, you can stream or download songs from the Xbox Music Store. You can also sync your music across multiple Windows 8 devices and the Xbox 360.

- ▸ **Manage Music Devices.** Add or change devices that can access your Music Pass.

- ▸ **Redeem Code.** Enter a code to redeem items from Xbox Live, Music Pass, and more.

- ▸ **Manage Payment Options.** Change or add credit card billing information.

- ▸ **Billing Contact Information.** Change or add billing information.

- ▸ **Billing History.** Internet Explorer is launched, and a log-in window in the browser prompts you to enter your Microsoft account and password so you can view billing history.

- ▸ **Privacy and Online Settings.** This setting opens an Internet Explorer window so you can sign in to Xbox, where you can change online and privacy settings.

- ▸ **Contact Preferences.** Tap this to receive or stop receiving Xbox newsletters.

G My Account settings

Confirm purchases

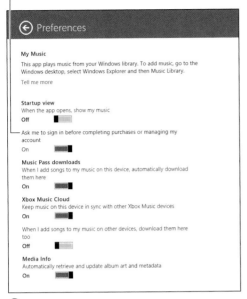

H Preferences settings

To change Preferences settings:

Use these settings to manage how the Music app works for you.

Access the Charms bar, tap Settings, and tap Preferences **H**.

- **My Music.** Tap the *Tell me more* link for help with how to add songs to the My Music folder.

- **Startup view.** Drag the slider to On to have the Music app open the My Music folder when it launches.

- **Confirm purchases.** Drag the slider to On to receive a prompt before completing a music purchase.

- **Music Pass downloads.** Drag the slider to On to automatically download songs to the tablet.

- **Xbox Music Cloud.** Drag the slider to On to sync music on the tablet with other Xbox Music devices, and to add music downloaded on other Xbox Music devices to the tablet.

- **Media Info.** Drag the slider to On to retrieve or update album art and song metadata.

To change privacy settings:

You can turn Notifications on and off.

1. Access the Music app's Charms bar, tap Settings, and then tap Permissions.

2. Drag the slider on or off to receive or prevent notifications 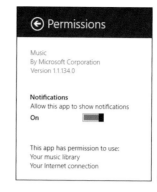.

TIP To search for a song using the Search charm, type the name of the song instead of the artist.

TIP Xbox Music Pass is the new version of Microsoft's previous music service, Zune Music Pass.

⬅ Permissions

Music
By Microsoft Corporation
Version 1.1.134.0

Notifications
Allow this app to show notifications

On

This app has permission to use:
Your music library
Your Internet connection

ⓘ Notifications

Maps

Are you always looking for directions? The Maps app on the Surface tablet will help you find your way. It has opt-in options for setting your location so you can quickly find things nearby, or you can turn it off if you're trying to find a location that's not in your immediate area.

Maps are available in two views: aerial and road, so you can get as much or as little detail as you'd like. You can swipe to move maps around the screen.

Map Views

There are two map views: Aerial and Road. Aerial view is a satellite map. Road view displays streets as well as landmarks such as train stations and neighborhood names. Both views support the Show Traffic option. The Maps app can be snapped so it can be viewed while using other apps.

To change the map view:

1. Tap the Maps tile on the Start screen.

2. Swipe down from the top or up from the bottom of the tablet to display the Maps app bar Ⓐ.

Ⓐ Maps app bar

3. Tap Map Style on the app bar, and tap Aerial View **B** or Road View **C**.

B Aerial view

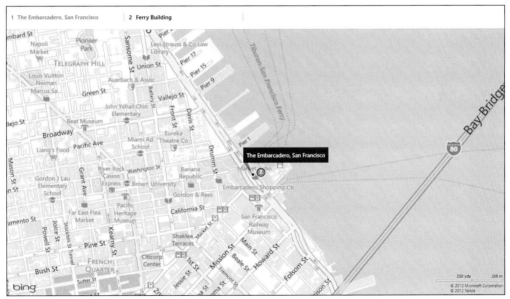

C Road view

To display traffic:

1. Swipe up from the bottom edge of the Maps screen to display the app bar.

2. Tap Show Traffic .

D Traffic shown in Road view

To view Maps in other apps:

1. With the Maps app running, tap the Windows button at the base of the tablet to return to the Start screen, and select the app you want to have Maps appear in.

2. To reveal the left-side panel, swipe in from the left.

3. Slowly drag Maps toward the center of the screen until you see the divider bar, and then release to snap the Maps app into a third of the screen **E**.

4. Drag the divider bar toward the right side of the screen, and release when Maps takes up about two-thirds of the screen **F**.

TIP Pinch to zoom in or reverse-pinch to zoom out on a map.

TIP Show Traffic works in both Aerial view and Road view.

TIP Access the Search charm and tap Maps to search for a location when viewing Maps within another app.

E Maps appearing alongside News

F Maps appearing on the left side of the screen

Locating Places and Getting Directions

You can use Maps to get directions to and from a location. As of this writing, there is no support for directions to multiple destinations. Finding a location requires using the Search charm or tapping the Find button in the Maps app bar. Getting directions requires using the app bar.

To set your location:

When you first open Maps, you'll be prompted with a request to access your location. (Tap the Block button if you don't want your location saved.)

1. Access the Settings charm, and tap Permissions.

2. Drag the Location slider to the right.

To find your location on a map:

1. Swipe up from the bottom of the Maps screen to display the app bar.

2. Tap the My Location button. Your physical location appears on the map.

To add a pin to a map:

1. Swipe up from the bottom of the Maps screen to display the app bar.

2. Drag the Add a Pin button to a place on the map where you want to add a pin. A yellow dot appears on the map.

3. Tap the pin to get the address of the pinned location. You can also tap the Directions button to get directions to or from the pin's location. Tap the Remove button to delete the pin from the map.

1	**Barnes & Noble Inc** 122 5th Ave Fl 2, New York, NY (212) 253-0810
2	Barnes & Noble 105 5th Ave Frnt 1, New York, NY (212) 253-0810
3	Barnes & Noble 76 9th Ave Fl 9, New York, NY (212) 414-6000
4	Barnes & Noble 396 Avenue Of The Americas, New ... (212) 674-8780
5	Barnes & Noble 227 W 27th St, New York, NY (212) 594-0359
6	Barnes & Noble 4 Astor Pl, New York, NY (212) 420-1322
7	Barnes & Noble 555 5th Ave Frnt B, New York, NY
8	Barnes & Noble 97 Warren St, New York, NY (212) 267-3474
9	Barnes & Noble

Ⓐ Viewing more results

To search for a location:

1. Swipe in from the right side of the Map screen, and tap Search on the Charms bar.

   or

   Swipe up from the bottom of the screen to access the app bar, and tap Find.

2. Enter the location (business name or street address) in the text box in the right pane, and tap the Search icon to the right of the text box. The location appears on the map with an address and phone number, along with Directions and Website buttons. If there is more than one location for a business you're searching, blue numbered circles appear on the map. Tap one to get information about the location.

3. Tap the down arrow in the upper-left corner of the screen to see other search results Ⓐ.

4. To change the search criteria, tap the Refine Your Search button, and add more detailed location information Ⓑ.

Ⓑ Refining a search

To get directions:

1. On the Maps app bar, tap Directions.

2. Type a start location in **A** and an end location in **B**, and then tap the right-facing arrow **C**.

3. Tap the double-arrow icon to reverse the directions **C**.

C Getting directions

TIP Enter as much information as possible when using the Maps Search charm.

TIP If you do not have your physical location set on the tablet and you're searching for places nearby, be sure to enter your city and state when searching for a location or directions.

TIP If you have already used Search to find a location, you'll only need to enter a starting point to get directions.

TIP You can also get directions once you find a location on the map by tapping the Directions button in the location detail box.

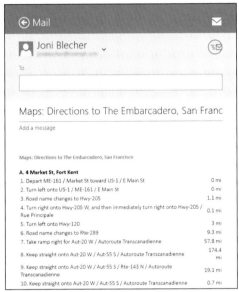

Using Charms with the Maps App

The Search, Share, Settings, and Devices charms work with Maps. Use the Settings charm to set your location (see "To set your location," in the previous section), change map regions, clear search history, display distance, and set some map usage controls. Use the Search charm to find a location on the map (see the previous section). Use the Share charm to share directions and maps with others. The Devices charm lets you send a map to connected devices.

To share directions with others:

1. Access the Charms bar, and tap Share **A**.

2. Tap Mail on the Share charm **B**.

3. Enter the email address for the contact you want to send the directions to, and tap the Send button in the message panel.

To print maps:

1. Access the Charms bar, and tap Devices **C**.

2. Tap the printer to which you want to print, and tap Print in the Devices panel.

A Share charm

B Emailing directions

C Devices charm

To change map settings:

Access the Charms bar, tap Permissions, and tap the *Options* link .

- **Change app region.** Tap the down arrow and swipe up or down in the pop-up to scroll through regional locations. Tap the region you want.

- **Search history.** Drag the slider to the right to turn on search history.

- **Clear search history.** Tap this button to remove your recent map searches.

- **Show distance in.** Display distance in either kilometers or miles.

- **Angled view of aerial map.** Drag the slider to the right to turn on the ability to view aerial maps at an angle.

- **Zoom.** Drag the slider to the right to show zoom controls on the map.

TIP If your location setting is off, be as specific as possible when entering a search term in the Search charm.

D Map settings

Index